Life's Pages

A Book of Poetry;
People, Places, and Things

David J. Gluck

iUniverse, Inc.
New York   Bloomington

Life's Pages
A Book of Poetry; People, Places, and Things

iUniverse books may be ordered through booksellers or by contacting:

iUniverse
1663 Liberty Drive
Bloomington, IN 47403
www.iuniverse.com
1-800-Authors (1-800-288-4677)

ISBN: 978-1-4401-0651-4 (sc)
ISBN: 978-1-4401-0652-1 (ebook)

Library of Congress Control Number: 2008943689

Printed in the United States of America

iUniverse rev. date: 1/7/2009

Table of Contents

Preface

Different writer's have different reasons for writing. Some wish to be persuasive, others want to explore their imagination, and there are those who wish to record history. David Gluck has managed to create a combination of all these previous qualities, including the ability to challenge thought. Life's Pages includes the people, places, and things that affected his life in various ways. With a unique style he has superbly recorded these events to share with you. The poetry that follows in these pages is a perception of one man's mind that has managed to find its way here. Since you have found your way here as well, open your mind and enjoy.

For my mom who always told
me to get this out there…I wish
she was still here to see it.

I'm a Poet, if You Must

Some may think that I'm a writer; some may think I'm opinionated,
Others may think I'm an opinionated writer, but what do they know?
I'm a poet, if you must!

My politics don't matter and neither does my religion, education, eliteness or lack thereof,
Society need not know whether I was black, white, rich, poor, national or foreign.
It need not matter whether I loved women, men, both or neither,
Whether I was friend or foe to you and yours or theirs.

Some may say that for purpose of art I put words together, but I am not an artist, from them I draw my words.
The beauty of their paintings, drawings, sculptures, architecture, landscaping and destruction are the conversations of these pages.

There are those that may think I desire fame and fortune by making music out of my words, further from the truth they couldn't be and the reason is simple,
These words at that point would only be temporary without chance of lasting throughout the ages.

They call me conservative, liberal, right winger, left winger, ideological, philosophical, idealistic, indecisive, moronical,

They add to that straight, gay, homophobic, religious, theistic, atheistic, Christian, Jew, Muslim, dirt.
They say that I am immoral, elite, too poor to have a thought,
I have no vision or worthiness,
I haven't the value of the educators, politicians, preachers, studied, well versed.
To them I say, "say what you will and draw your own conclusions. Then turn the pages of this book so that I may also connect to you."
See, my goal is not to thrive on fortune and fame or drive home some non-important contemporary view.
I strive to reach out to those in need in the most important way and showing them they're not alone.
I strive to reach across societal boundaries and connect with all of humanity.
That is who I am and what I do,
I am a poet, if you must!

Dreaming

"Hey Babe," I heard the wind calling to me,
"Let's go somewhere today and be free."
"Ok," I said and we were off.
First stop, the Neirstein Bahnhof.

"Why," asked the wind, "are we stopping here?"
"Because," I replied, "this place can get us far and near."
"Fine, I guess you won't be needing me anymore today.
I could've taken you places and you wouldn't have had
    to pay."

"How's that?" I asked this time.
Once again it replied, "Not even a dime."
"Ok, ok, you've got me hooked!"
"Close your eyes for a sec, then you can look."

I did what it said without hesitation,
The next thing I knew was a miraculous sensation.
In the air I was and without any wings,
Hearing almost nothing, except the birds sing.

I was filled with questions and awe,
Mostly 'cause this defies every law.
The wind must have known I had things to ask.
"Don't worry," it said, "this is a simple task."

I kept quiet as we continued on our way.
It then was getting late, the wind exclaimed, "I must go,
    I can't stay!"
I said, "That's fine," and it took me back.
"I'll return when I have no clouds to pack."

"Go to sleep and you will see
That what you experienced wasn't me."
So, up I went to find my bed,
When I awoke, I understood, it was all in my head.

Life

Gliding across the water on a hot summer day
Or working in the field bailing hay.
Relaxing on a shoreline waiting for a bite,
Or riding down the highway on a 10 speed bike.
Driving a truck across the country,
Or just picking some leaves off a great big tree.
Going out on the town with your lady,
Or watching a flower being pollinated by a bee.

All of these are a part of life.
You need excitement and you need strife.
Don't be afraid of what lies ahead
And don't waste your life by staying in bed.
Get out in the world and go explore,
There are many things to do, rich or poor.
Don't live your life moaning and groaning,
Instead, live it happy and constantly roaming.

(No Title)

How can you love something that can't love you back?
At the same time hate it so much because everything it
    seems to lack.
Freedom is yours, to do as you please
But this relationship is just one big tease.
Within it, there's a new face everyday
However, to any one of them, there is nothing to say.
Always at home, it seems, but never where you want to be,
Constantly serving others first, seldom worrying about me.
Here and there, somewhere different all the time
Forever hoping the sounds will continue to rhyme.
The true meaning of a "love/hate relationship,"
You bet, at times, on my shoulder there is a chip.
There are other places sometimes I'd rather be,
For starters, near a bathroom when I gotta pee.
Birthdays and Easter, Fourth of July,
Christmas, Thanksgiving…sometimes I cry.

(No Title)

"When are you coming home?"
Ever get use to being all alone?
"Can you take us to the park?"
I've gotten use to being in the "dark."
"I want you to play with us outside."
Kids are too young in whom to confide.
"Will you buy us something at the store?"
Always, it seems, I'm striving for something more.

Loneliness

Loneliness is a strange thing.
No matter how many people you know
And how often the telephone may ring,
Alone in this world, still you go.

People, no matter what, are only temporary.
Even surrounded by many friends
And, if and when you decide to marry
The emptiness still never ends.

Being surrounded by people is nice
It gives our minds a chance to rest.
However, individuality has a high price,
For our minds, this price is loneliness.

Blinding Sight

How different my life would surely be
If the things around me I could not see.
Flowers and trees, the clouds in the sky,
Valleys and rivers, the mountains so high.
Dogs and cats, the cows in the fields,
Cars and trucks, the signs that say yield.
Red and green, the black of the night,
Blue and orange, the morning daylight.
Your eyes and nose, the hair on your head,
Your fingers and toes, your lips, which are red.
I thank God for this gift that He gave to me,
A good pair of eyes, so all things I may see.

Home

San Francisco on a foggy morn,
Miami and Tampa during a storm.
Hot and dry in Phoenix all year,
Perfect in Hawaii, I only hear.
Seattle and Portland, the northwest is nice,
Going through Nevada? Roll the dice.
LA is huge with a whole lot to do,
Sets, the beach, and even a zoo.
Laredo, Dallas, Kansas City, and St. Paul,
I-35 runs through the middle of them all.
Unique is Chicago, just south of the lake,
Cars in Detroit, that's what they make.
St. Louis is cool coming in from the east,
The riverfront there is an awesome beast.
Rivers and hills, music and Memphis,
Tennessee is a state not to be missed.
What do I say about Wyoming?
Hang onto your hat, the winds always blowing.
Indy is fast, yes, they like to race,
On 465, ya better pick up the pace.
Cincinnati, their Bengal's, better days they have seen,
But there is a reason this town's called the Queen.
By the lake in the mountains you have Coeur 'de Alene,
Up in north Idaho, it sure isn't lame.
Philadelphia, its ports are home for "the bell,"
Three rivers in Pittsburgh, steel is their sell.
Mississippi has Tupelo, home to "the king,"
Yea, Elvis down there, did learn to sing.
A peach is Atlanta, known as "big A,"
New York, the "big apple," stands proud to this day.

Fond of their past are Dodge City and Meade.
The Midwest is known for the people they feed.
Gallup and Tulsa are known for their kicks,
They're on that old highway, route 66.
Charleston is buried in mountains of coal,
New Orleans is a city which is full of soul.
Washington, DC, represented by more than one face,
From all around they come to this place.
New England is different it seems to me,
Peaceful and quiet, a nice place to be.
Chapel Hill and Ft. Collins, universities they boast,
To all of America, I'll make a toast;
Across the home of the brave and the land of the free,
Every bit of this great country, is home to me.

The Storm

The clouds are billowing in the sky
Over the prairie, a mile high.
The winds have picked up and the dust blows
How bad will it be, no one knows.

The days been hot from dawn until dusk
The air smells different, a new musk.
If winter it was, fog it would be
But now it is spring, storms I see.

Thunder rolling and everyone hears
Children now running, with new fears.
People rushing to find their way home
Now even our pets, end their roam.
Lightning strikes like fingers from above

The sky to the ground, shocking love.
Our lights go out and candles we find
Except for a flash, we are blind.

Windows now rattle from bass so strong
Little ones frightened, sing a song.
Under a blanket the dog now hides
Across the prairie, thunder glides.

The sky is falling and rain comes down
All streets are flooded, in our town.
We stay inside and hope for just rain
If hail should fall…cause more pain.

The ground is dry so with rain this hard
All washing away, is my yard.
Water is needed but storms are not
Now cooling outside, it was hot.
The storms now passed but powers still out,
With Mother Nature, one more bout.
A mess we have laying on the ground
Clean up tomorrow, all around.

Soldiering

Surrounded by many yet feel all alone
My duty carries me far from home.
Been trained to fight yet struggle to stay alive
Courage and honor won't let me take a dive.
Freedom you have far away from where I am
My country is why I fight for Uncle Sam.

Politics

A tool used to divide friends.
A tool used to divide families.
A tool used to divide the Church.
A tool used to divide industry.

More than just a word, it intrudes on one's beliefs.
More than just a person, it intrudes on a nation's sovereignty.
More than just a nation, it invades all the world's societies.
Bigger than all the world, its corrupting wake encompasses the earth.

It begins by censoring speech,
It continues by controlling thought,
It makes you think you need it to survive,
It counts on fear by all people for its success.

It uses the people in all governments to thwart its control.
It doesn't matter the persons or parties involved.
It misleads the people throughout all societies
So its laws can be imposed.

A single government of its own is ultimately the goal.
Relentlessly striving for power so it can rule the world.
It's not a person, religion, or group of people which seem to be the enemy,
Instead, it's a powerful word which will conquer by dividing all.
Politics.

Dusk

Late afternoon and the sun's in my eyes.
Making me tired, my body wants to lie.
Blocking it out the best that I can,
The visors too short so I use my hand.
Forcing myself to stay awake
Through my hair my fingers rake.
Behind the cloud it hides for a while,
Not long enough, only a mile.
North nor south nor heading east,
Only west is it this beast.
The clouds are few but the horizon's close,
A shot of cold air, I take a dose.
Middle of the windshield it's officially centered,
 A couple more miles and dusk will be entered.
The ground finally catches the sun,
Another day is almost done.
This is the most awesome time it seems,
Up into the clouds, the sun, it beams.
Colors galore, from pink to blue,
Goodbye for today, from the sun to you.

My Reply

With a look of disbelief in her eyes,
"You moved back to Shen, why?"
Not able to understand me back in the town where we
    grew up
I explained, "It's the only place where I have a full cup."

Critically shaking her head, she started to walk away,
"Lend me your ears for a moment and I'll tell you why
    I stay."

Off to Europe I went after graduating high school,
Through Paris and Amsterdam acting like a damn fool.
Living in wine country on the Rhine in Germany,
October in Munich spent partying with many.
A field in Luxemburg where Patton watches his men to
    this day,
A town called Garmish where in '72 the Olympians
    played.
Visited Dachau, one of many horrors of World War II,
Skied Austria and Switzerland, white water rafted there
    too.
Ate at Maria's downtown in Oppenheim,
Always the best schnitzel, every single time.
When that was all over back home I came again,
Now more determined to go to places I hadn't yet been.

A year later the smell of change was in the air,
Around the country in a truck, to me that seemed fair.
I went to school and learned to jam gears,
Only twenty-one, I didn't have any fears.
At home one last time with a U-Haul full of gas
I piled in my things and drove off to north Kansas.
Next to Ft. Lauderdale, from there to Salt Lake,
Soon learning for a home, much time I couldn't make.
Seattle to Miami, Los Angeles to Maine
And everywhere in between, nothing's ever the same.
Hurricanes, earthquakes, tornados and floods,
It seems in every state now, I've spilled a little blood.

Saw the World Trade Center Towers before they fell,
A hundred times now, been through the home of the
    Liberty Bell.
Seen alligators crossing the road deep down in the south.
The Mississippi River in New Orleans, it has a big mouth.
The Missouri River starts at Three Forks in Montana,
Drove through the mountains from there all the way to
    Fontana.
Las Vegas and Seattle each have a space needle,
Seen the devastation caused by the infamous Bark Beetle.

With my everyday home sitting behind the wheel
And forty-eight states from which to choose my next meal
When I go home I want comfort and space,
And room to play, my kids need a place.
Extended family and friends are there waiting for me
If it wasn't my home, my kids I'd never see.
Maybe someday when I'm old and my kids have moved
    away
I could retire in Montana or near Chesapeake Bay.
I've lived in Missouri, California, and K. C.,
In each their own way, they've been decent to me,
But my cup started filling a long time ago
And I've watched people leave, both friend and foe.
For many years now, Shen's been poured into my cup,
With children and friends, it's been all filled up,
And with all of the place's I've had a chance to roam,
Shenandoah is the only one I wish to call home.

Politicians

Their quest for prosperity has screwed up our lives,
It slashes our souls like six foot knives.
No longer do they believe that survival is key,
"Who cares about you, it's all about me!"
They scratch and they claw and they fight for wealth,
They sell their souls and they neglect our health.
"I'm better than you," is a common tone.
Like the wolf on the prairie, we must go it alone.
They've got something to prove but to whom does it
    matter?
There are those without food while the rich grow fatter.
Redistribution of wealth may not be the answer
But it shouldn't cost thousands to treat those with cancer.
They "all knowingly" try to solve problems around the
    world
While here at home children, under bridges, are curled.
Claiming, "I care about you," to office they're elected
But once on "The Hill" their core is neglected.
I'm pissed at politicians for sending billions abroad
And shunning their own without even a nod.

The Fly on the Wall?

Sometimes people wish that they could be me
So they could observe the things that I see.
Wondering "why," that thought blows me away,
Most things that I see they fight to keep at bay.
I see and hear things with no means to understand

My life is spent searching for a good place to land.
Cat food then feces', hey dinner is served!
Shew'd from the table around their hand I swerve,
I land on their glass then on the dog's nose.
Next go searching for food in their dirty clothes.
Kitchen's and bathroom's are my favorite two rooms
Sticky and smelly, and dirty old brooms.
Them walls are just boundaries they're no place for me
The over full trash can, mmmmm, that's where I'll be!

America's Poet

I am moved as *The Captain* says "So Long."
He's become my friend; his words are more; his soul still
    ventures on.
His life was just and worthy while writing of this land,
The wars, the growth, the vastness protruded through his
    hand.
He spoke of love and hate and death; of birth and love
    some more,
He found the good inside the souls and dreamed of peace
    not war.
His style was not to rhyme or bounce, just write what
    came to him,
He loved the sea and *Leaves of Grass*, his notes became
    the hymn.

Dreaming of the most perfect mothers birthing a hundred
    millions of superb persons denoting America,
Expressing to all – black and white, male and female, Indian
    and Hispanic – to make real the dream America.

He told each man and woman to have confidence in
   themselves,
He told each child, both boy and girl, to embrace America
   ourselves.
He praised this land he called his home and lived through
   it divided,
He kept his notes all through this time until again United.
He loved the union of these states and dreamed they
   would stay strong,
He loved Mannahatta – the island town – dear subject
   of his song.
To soldiers both from north and south he gave to them
   their due,
Their spirits seemed to then thank him; at peace united
   too.
Believing in his country, strong and bold, renewed again
   undivided, promoting its freedom to all,
Around the world jocund he sang – America will stand tall!
He reached out to you and people like me in hope of
   inspiring great thought,
He desired more poets to come along to expand on his
   leaves; their seeds having been caught.

He wrote of all that America was and wished for her to
   grow,
He foresaw great power and wars to come, her prominence
   in the world he seemed to know.
Her rivers, mountains, lakes, plains, and sea; he loved
   them all the same,
But Her mothers and sailors and soldiers to him were
   most deserving of history's fame.

He understood his place in time and accepted his position,
The legacy he left for us was not one of acquisition,
His songs to us carry more weight as history's tongue
    than gold in all the earth,
And his death, to him, was not the end, instead a new life
    through birth.
The Captain says, *so long*!
(*Whispering his love and blowing a kiss, so long!*)

Sounds of Heaven

I close my eyes and listen to the sounds of heaven,

        The children laugh,
        The musician sings,
        The squirrels chase,
        The golf club swings,
        The carp rollick,
        The sea gently laps,
        The air horns sound,
        The thunder claps.

The leaves rustle in the wind,
And big trucks hum smoothly down streets of gold.

Echo's

Atop the canyon I peer down,
It is silent and I am alone.
The canyon is narrow; the colors are abundant.
I now hear the river below as it rages; it echo's from the
    bottom of the canyon.
I am compelled to explore.

I look to my left; I look to my right.
It appears there is no way down.
The edge is steep; a path is spotted.
I make my way to the floor below not thinking about
    returning.

A clearing, the river is calm and silent, the rocks are
    arranged invitingly.
There is shelter from a cave open to this area.
Strangely, wildlife is nonexistent.
I stumble, the noise is deafening, it continues uninterrupted.
I tell it to stop, it tells me to stop.
I scream, it screams back.
I yell louder, it returns the favor.
The river no longer is peaceful; the canyon is insane.
The noise is disorienting; I begin talking to myself.
The walls now talk as well.
No longer am I compelled to explore.
From the floor of the canyon I peer up.
The rocks are crying and I am alone.

The Eyes Who View

Society suggests I must be sad,
Alone through time, life must be bad,
With no one there to share my day,
No loving body with which to lay,
No lips to kiss goodbye each morn,
No hand to hold when mind is torn,
No love to share through passing time,
No one to console, perceived as mine.
I would suggest society doesn't know,
Each part it seems has its *highs* and *lows*.
Are married couples more glad than I
Each alone in thought and burdened by
Pressure to please *the one* who makes them complete?
Stress abounds in those *jumping through hoops* to
    accomplish that feat.
And memories from a time when they were alone
Set anxiety high and minds to roam.
What ifs are asked inside their minds,
Dreams of new can sometimes blind.
They ask the opposite of society as I,
I'm perceived to be happy, why?

Sadness and happiness are labeled by a society which assumes
But perception is relative only to the eyes who view.

American

I don't know what it's like to be black, white, Asian,
Hispanic, Aussie, Philippine, or Middle Eastern.
I am not French, German, Italian, or British, nor am I
Polish, Spanish, Portuguese, Turkish, or Jew.
Norwegian, Swedish, Finnish, Irish, Hollander, Belgian,
Austrian, nor Swiss am I.
The Greek are proud people but one of them I'm not
either.
Moroccan, Sudanese, Liberian, Egyptian, Libyan,
Tanzanian, nor from South Africa am I.
Not Cuban, Mexican, Honduran, Argentine, Peruvian,
Chilean.
Not Palestinian, Jordanian, Syrian, Saudi, Iraqi, Iranian,
Afghan, Pakistani, nor Indian.
I hail not from Taiwan or China, Korea or Vietnam, nor
am I from Japan or Russia.
I am not Canadian, Columbian, nor Jamaican.
I am not any one part of the world, for I am made of all,
I am American!

Around the Room Gazing

Around the room gazing at strangers
Old, young, and in between
Time is only relevant to now
For I didn't know that man when his hair wasn't gray
Nor will I know that child when his hair is
What will the future bring to the innocence across the room
And how has the teachings of time transformed the old
    man who once was young?

Unfortunate Fools

Peace within is only temporary, sporadic at best.
Peace in the world is only an illusion, never complete.
Is there a relationship between peace individually and
    peace in the world?
Quite possibly, in that both maybe are not meant for this
    state of being.

We strive with our emotions, religions, employment, wealth
    and lack thereof to be content with our surroundings.
With that *accomplished* we say we are *at peace* with
    ourselves.
We are foolish.
Contentedness is only one step towards harmony; an
    enlightenment of being seems as if it must also be
    included.
Without enlightenment our souls continue to be in
    conflict with themselves.

One or more nations *force* another or more at *gun point* to
"negotiate peace" between themselves and/or others.
That only leaves animosity and war because no nation
seems to ever be completely satisfied with another.
Nations are more foolish.
Again, contentedness is only one step towards harmony;
an enlightenment of being seems as if it must also be
included.
Without enlightenment, world nations will continue to
be in conflict with themselves and each other.

My *Desire* is that peace fully encompassed would be possible.
Reason would lead me to believe it is attainable.
Knowledge, however, laughs at both.
The quest for peace is noble, what we embrace as peace
is foolish.

Most likely, peace is only accomplished in death, and that
could very well depend upon your living beliefs.
My belief is that most people will *NEVER* know what
true peace is all about.
That, is unfortunate.

Old Oak Tree

The sprawled out old oak tree on the hill,
Overlooking the town, it seems it always will,
It's been up there all alone since I can remember,
Springing to life in May, dormant in December,
Pushed to the brink by the bitter wind,
Through storms of life it has learned to bend,

As a guardian it stands proud and tall,
Its presence has touched us all,
Grandpa says it was old when he was young,
Still looking on, no one knew it would live this long,
As if on sacred ground,
It stands alone upon the mound,
No visitors have I ever seen,
To the tree, on the hill so green,
Only birds and bugs and squirrels up there,
Nothing in winter, it is so bare,
Sometimes wondering if it could use a friend,
To groom and care for it until the end,
It seems to whisper I am fine,
You people in town are friends of mine,
I've watched over your grandparents and theirs before,
I've watched you grow and I'll watch some more.
The old oak tree upon the hill,
Stands tall and proud, and always will.

Revolving Door

So, time can mend a broken heart, ain't that what they say?
Well, how much time? I ask them to tell me if they may.
Five years, ten years, twenty years or more,
Or do you just get stuck forever in this revolving door?

You think you get out for a minute but your mind is just
    fooled
Around your ankle is a bungee and back in, you it just pulled.
Now mopping the floor with you flat on your face,
This stupid door is laughing and calling you a disgrace.

Scratching your head as you try to regain your composure,
The contempt toward your heart is now growing more pure.
Finally back on your feet again, you're walking 'round
and 'round,
Thinking this time, *I'll get out; by my heart I'm not going
to be bound!*

You check for attachments and you run as fast as you can,
Without your heart, you're free, now you are a new man.
This running's your new life and so you pretend to live,
But true love to another, without a heart you can't give.

You go through all the motions and all the right words
you say,
With no meaning behind them, this game does end one day.
You run faster now and stride farther than before,
Away from your heart, not wanting to contend with the door.

Weary now after having run for so long,
Wondering why your life feels empty and what's wrong.
You stop for the first time thinking, *I need to get some rest,
For meaning and purpose, tomorrow is my new quest.*

You wake in the morning, even more tired than before,
Struggling and fighting to rise so you can run some more.
Slipping and falling because you are blind to where you
are going,
A hook from your heart, at you the revolving door is
throwing.

It snags onto your jeans and you rip it away,
You scoff at it and scream, *Ha! You won't get me today!*

Little did you know that that was only a deception,
The revolving door's waiting for your mopping reception.

Yes again your heart found you and with it now you must
    deal,
All the pain and the sorrow, the broken pieces you must
    seal.
Again, if time can mend a broken heart, how much will
    it take
To make me a real person, with a heart that's not fake?

Listen to One

I look around and observe a different population,
One that hides from society in part; a homeless situation.
People who have found hard times for one reason or another
Those who endure all elements thrown; along with all
    the weather.
Most people seem as if they're blind to those who are all
    around,
Not wishing to acknowledge the reality which obviously
    surrounds.
Talking with the *misfortuned tribe* I find a vast intelligence,
Bitterness towards prosperity is not the feeling that I
    sense.
A traumatic experience seems to have led each one of
    these people there,
Something I think we could understand if compassion
    would lend an ear.
A divorce or layoff, or family death; a feeling of no self
    worth,

Something of one we've all been through I'm sure, at least
   once since birth.
An ear to them is worth more than gold; dry socks worth
   more than food,
A smoke or some change and Christmas has come and
   thankful; they are not rude.
I press for *all* more fortunate than some to lend a helping
   hand,
Listen to one or two or three and *help* the homeless in
   our land.

I've Got to Wonder

I've got to wonder about the past I see,
Is it an accurate description for me?
And currently what about the spin on T.V.,
What will the future look back to see?

Trying to not get lost in the bliss of today
I dream of tomorrow, scratch my head and say,
Learn your lessons early in life,
Don't burden yourself with all this strife,
Don't fight and argue 'til your face turns blue,
Or be like us, you will too.

We have our passions and we like to fight.
We know not peace, be we left or right,
We spend our days and all our might,
Lost to ourselves having lost all sight.

Be true to yourselves forgetting not what's all around,
Your life is comprised of all that surrounds.
The other opinion will always abound,
So listen to all life's most important sounds.

I've got to wonder about the future I see,
Are we an example that's good for thee?
From homes to towns to States and D.C.,
We are full of disdain and lack civility.

A United Divide; polarized we now are,
The next will suffer; possibly still more.
An example of peace is not so hard to see,
Nature provides visions of harmony,
To look around while absorbing the sounds,
We *could* remember *the* lesson which completely surrounds.

Debate is good yet should not consume,
Our lives for that do not have room.
Life's treasures get lost with mind in that set,
Bitterness prevails and our future we forget.

Photo Book

A book of memories exists in my mind
Flushing them out I fight to find
A new beginning point in my mind.
Those photos are great but no longer are they
Necessary to relive and dwell on each day,
Their purpose is served and lessons well taught,
It's time to begin anew; fresh pictures are sought,

(To live is to learn; hard lessons bought.)
We repeat the mistakes we have not yet learned
By this vicious cycle my mind has now learned
Living in the past you continue to get burned.
New mistakes await my mind to see
Life will go on to be
Full of new bliss and glee.
Fresh photos will now fill my mind
Flipping through the old at times I will find
A happy time gone by amidst a present kind
Thrusting forward through time.
The old has its place in rhyme
The new its place is now I'm aware
With yesterdays dreams gone forever somewhere
Permanently unattainable and torturously unfair.
Here I am again not away from my mind
Wishing new pictures somewhere it could find
So the past no longer would torment and bind,
To forget would free my mind.
A delete button would sure be nice,
But even for that there would be a price,
For lessons would never be attained even made twice,
And forever in circles we'd still be caged mice.
However, life awaits to continue on
And in a few hours will come a new dawn
For mind to take snapshots of all that surrounds
In hopes of capturing that scene which will turn around
The photo book of memories and make now abound,
Click…

(No Title)

I wonder if she knew –
When – as a dove she flew
Away from dormant trees –
As if – an eagle – or a bee,
That one petal at a time –
The hill – as a rose – she climbed.

(No Title)

Her fate was such that she was unknown
Nestled beneath the oak tree
Except by a few she called her own,
Robin – rose – and bumble bee.

<u>Fetching</u>

Set here on a lowly pedestal
Looking up to the world around,
Searching for the words of thought
About an emotion I have found.

The emotion must become a thought
With words to express it clear,
Words so all the world,
This emotion inside may hear.

Appearance

Expound upon the expanded imagination,
Unbound the dreams that come.
Espouse novelty in all of great creation,
Dowse by pen; no more keep mum.

Beauty of surrounding is valid
So make beautiful the ballad
Of whatever it is you see,
To include the sore and wretchedly.

Idealize the ideal in all;
Make larger than life the fall!
A poet's job is not done right
Until a dream becomes sight.

So dream and dream and dream some more,
Let not your vision become a bore,
Open your eyes and examine the shore,
Allow your mind to plunge through the door.

Extricate surreal of the real.
Expound nothing less than ideal.
(Drive the pen to promote the dream,
On paper – perfection – make it seem.)

(No Title)

Don't need to rhyme per-fect-ly,
Don't need to rhyme at all,
Only need the pen to see
The thought on which it calls.

Season of Reason

Our nature is to reason,
Yet answers are never in season.
Yeah, we may know *some* things;
Create little ditty's that tingle and sting,
Pretend to know why things are,
Pretend that we are the only star,
Walk around all confident from place to place,
(With a stupid self-righteous smile upon our face)
Giving answers to anyone who asks,
Remaining ourselves confused by our own tasks.
We think we're gods to direct our own plight
Yet with each barrier we continue to fight
Knowing we don't understand.
Larger, it seems, is the hand
Which seems to understand reason
(For us answers are not in season).
We fight with God to understand
Demanding He send throughout the land
The secrets we *think* we must know.
It's almost like God just keeps telling us where to go,
(Figuratively speaking of course, until judgment day at least)
And on Him, our angers feast.
Now, I'm not certain *that* anger's displaced
But God's in control of all things placed
In this path of life we're on.
Sometimes I feel like a pawn,
Being bounced between good and bad;
By this game, having been had;
Left not to understand;
Blind to the controlling hand;

Lost between the seasons of reason,
Wondering if answers will ever be in season.
Wondering, wondering, wondering I am,
(Now I sound like *Sam I am*)
But getting nowhere I've not been it seems,
As with how the infinite serpent dreams
Of spitting out its tail.
Are we doomed to fail?
Will the answers ever fall
Upon us so we can end our call?
No. God's purpose would then cease to be,
For no one would then call on He
To comfort and sort things out.
All call on Him? That I doubt
And they will either stop or go
Most likely understanding they don't know
But coming to an understanding either way.
Even those who do are confused I must say
For nothing even then makes sense.
The season of reason is awfully dense,
More so than pea soup.
(Like the serpent, I continue to loop.)
Confused is the reason for the season
Of trying to learn how to reason.
Infinity at its best,
For reason is the quest
And something we probably will never find
At least while on earth 'til the end of our time.
Was Job ever to understand
He was a pawn protected by God's hand?
His faith was strong and remained so through
The torment and torment that Satan blew

Upon him day after day.
He is a saint, I say if I may,
Never questioning he kept on with God 'til the end,
He did not sway or bend,
Only accepted that God knew what He was doing.
Today we'd all be suing!
Maybe we might all accept our fate,
Use the tools that God left at the gate
And sweep to Him our instinct to reason,
Understanding that for us, answers are not in season.

Nature calls

Lightning strikes somewhere near
Its flash I see; thunder I hear
Drops of rain now start to fall
Even in nature; nature calls
It bellows its sounds from within itself
It blows my papers off the shelf
If fills the ponds; lakes, rivers and streams,
(Indigestion enormous it seems!)

Turtle

I would like to be a turtle.
Able to retreat any time to my shell,
To escape the seemingly earthly hell
Which blocks my path as hurdles.
Oh, to be a turtle is a dream of mine,
Retract and hide at anytime,
No wants, few needs, no expectations,
No reason for any misconceptions,
Responsibility for nothing else but me,
With even that slight for me to be,
(A turtle – not worried about the hurdle!)

The Horse Trots On

My reality changes as I begin to write,
No longer are traffic and people interacting with my mind,
I block the music out so I am not locked into time,
My thoughts again wander, the illusion created is soothing.

There's a dog, a cat, a mouse and a horse,
Playing in the field they are oblivious to me,
I watch the mouse taunt the cat, it jumps,
The dog barks and chases the cat,
The horse just stands there watching unimpressed.

A saddle is resting on the fence; I ease towards it
    unknowingly,
I am eyed and the horse comes to see,
Friendly, this creature appearing eager to carry nudges at
    the saddle,
We go for a ride.
This horse has a mind of its own; I have no control,
The dog, cat, and mouse are running along with us as
    they continue to play,
The path is well traveled, the horse knows its way,
It takes me here and there and back again, somewhat in
    circles it seems, going everywhere, yet nowhere at all,
It takes me on a trip through time.

The horse begins to trot.

The first stage of this excursion is one I'm most familiar with,
Filled with excitement, strife, happiness and sorrow,

Love, hate, fear, eagerness, curiosity, apprehension, despair,
    pride,
The trip of my own journey through time.

With no order, events jump out as warranted.
A snowstorm is raging, it is night, my daughter is born,
A hot summer morn, to the hospital we go, it's now
    afternoon, my son is born,
Joy and fear fill me, pride exudes.

I am in green on the Rhine; in a tent in Munich; the
    Eiffel Tower, then Holland; see General Patton and
    his men; smell the horror at Dachau…

The horse trots on.

It's the second of July, I see a courtroom, we are getting
    married,
It is now dark, though it is spring, I am divorced,
From elation to heartbreak, one scene I was shown.

I am on the steps, my children and parents are there;
    Mickey was met today,
The fireworks captivate and awe them,
It is a feeling I cannot explain; I struggle to hold the tears,
    they prevail.

It is raining; I'm frustrated and tired,
The TV is on the floor, the cooler has flown to the back,
    a small pick-up is under my hood; he is bloody and
    does not move,
They save him; I am distraught.

The horse trots on.

The scenes keep coming,
It is white; there are mountains all around,
Earlier today my eyes were crying as we said goodbye,
My hands now freeze; first time I've seen snow,
We drive in it to Iowa; New Year adventure for us all,
We are fine.
The dog now leaps from a rock onto my lap; Lou rides
    with me as I truck around,
Lou is gone, now Roxy rides,
The cat chases the dog back to the ground, fearless
    Whiskers waits for me by the door,
Anguish fills my heart.

A hospital at a time when I was young; Tina went down
    the hill without brakes on my encouragement,
Shame and guilt punish me.

A different hospital a few years later; Mom is sick,
Months go by; she is well,
Thank God.

A tree and a pile of snow, like the mouse, the other kids
    and I burrow,
A sense of peace comes over me.

The horse trots on.

I see faces flashing in the mist; Howard, Wendy, Max, Kimi,
Shawn, Jason, Mark, Sandy, Terry, Dave, Jill, Jon, Becky,
    Lori, Brad,

They keep sliding by; Mom, Dad, Tina, Mike, Angie, Paul,
   Jim, Ed, Joe,
Bob, Bill, Chris, Dan, Donnie, Barbara, Matt, Holly,
The show gets more intense, it doesn't seem as if it will end;
   Dee, Brenda, Gary, Amy, Tim, Kelly, Jennifer, Ron,
   Diane, Alexandra, Sean,
Mabel, Marsha, Jeff, David, Darrel, Michelle, Scott, Gwen,
   Mary, Steve,
Andre, Duane, Debbie, Shantel, Sheena…only the
   beginning of the faces I see,
Dean, Pat, Peg, Angel, Brian…the list goes on as my life
   flashes by…
I am filled with every emotion imaginable.
The horse trots on.

The scenes are compassionate and disheartened, funny
   and sad, filled with pride and shame,
I stand up for my beliefs; I just stand there and turn my head,
There are times I care and make a difference; there are
   times I don't, still making a difference,
The consequences of all my actions and inactions are
   significant to me and everyone around me,
Every scene in my life is shown to me as I ride,
My future is unclear; they cease in Sacramento with my
   birth.

The horse trots on.
The dog, cat, and mouse no longer play.

I am at the base of a hill; people are gathered all around,
There is chaos and order, hatred and sympathy,
A man walks by, I am filled with reverence, it is Christ,

He is crucified before my eyes; guilt…oh the naked guilt,
He ascends to Heaven and salvation is mine if I choose.

I am in an ancient house in Greece,
Plato records as Socrates debates Justice with friends,
The conversation is intense and enlightening; it lasts through
time.

The horse trots on.

There are frontiersmen and Indians,
The battles rage as the quest for land conquers and a
nation grows.

I am in New York, D.C., and Pennsylvania,
Planes, fire, devastation,
War continues today.

The dust is everywhere,
Crops won't grow, ragged clothes, no shoes, little food,
no money,
Depression; people persist, the nation thrives.

There is a play,
The President is here,
A loud noise, confusion breaks out, the leader is shot in
the head; he dies,
Mourning is National.

I am in a hall, it is vast and filled with Greatness,
These men are bickering amongst themselves, one is writing,
Independence is declared; a nation is born.

The bombs – oh the bombs – they are massive,
The horse trots on.

I am now in a place before time,
No light, no dark, nothing exists if that is possible,
As if commanded there is light,
There is dark, stars, sun, planets, life…God,
I am unworthy.

I am surrounded by influence,
Einstein, Aristotle, Moses, Plato, Abraham, Socrates,
   David; Job in all his despair,
Mathew, Mark, Luke, John; Christ lives in this place,
Lenin, Napoleon, Chamberlin, Stalin, Hitler, Churchill,
   Roosevelt,
Jefferson, Washington, Madison, Columbus, Lincoln
   and Reagan,
King, McCarthy, Nixon, Kennedy, Parks,
Custer, Red Beard, Donner,
Mozart, Bach, and Sinatra and Davis; Presley, Holly, Valens,
   and Ray,
Morrison even shows his face at this time,
Sonny makes music,
Hank and his bottle still cry,
There's Chaplin, Abbot, Disney, and Costello; Wayne,
   Rogers, and Trigger; Candy, Bellushi, and Andy; Winters
   and Carson,
Poe, Whitman, Bradbury, Orwell, Dickinson and Darwin;
   Melville, Freud, Dickens, Robinson, Shakespeare,
   Homer, and Webster; Twain, Stoker, and Pritchett.

I am filled with awe as the horse trots on.

All of history now floods my eyes; my relevance is revealed,
The ominous mountain, though it sustains life, hasn't the
    influence on individuals, society, or the world such as
    people have expelled,
May my influence be relevant; may it be Just and useful.

The horse trots no more.

We are back in the field where we began,
The mouse taunts the cat, it jumps,
The dog barks and chases the cat,
The horse just stands there watching unimpressed,
It is as if I am no longer there,
I watch a while and turn; they are gone.

A Subconscious Reality

A subconscious reality waits for me to sleep,
An illusion within anticipates my participation,
I close my eyes, unaware of the agenda,
I begin to dream…

> I am comfortable and happy,
> I am not shy or insecure,
> I am bold and assertive,
> I am not alone.

At first the scenes skip around,
They finally settle,
Not only is she physically gorgeous; she is completely
    beautiful,
The face of an angel, the dreamy body of perfection, the
    complimentary soul of my completion,
This is…
The alarm sings for the new day which awaits my arrival
    to its reality.
Some of my dreams drive me crazy,
They place me in situations which are not real,
They fill me with hope, happiness, joy, love,
They leave me longing for a different reality when I awaken,
They fill me with a consuming desire which is depressing.

The most beautiful woman in love with me and I with her,
The most perfect loving relationship,
This concept in itself is but a dream,
I wonder if it can really exist,
Before I again become conscious it seems it does for a while,

I only hope to escape from my reality back to the one I
    just came from,
It is no use; I cannot force my mind to go back there,
I must only wait for a time when my dreams carry me
    back there on their own,
Meanwhile, I must endure this depressing reality that all
    I have is this dream for now.

It seems as if this reality only exists in my dreams,
It makes me want to sleep and slip away forever,
I wish I could make this my true reality, instead of that
    which only exists in my mind,
If only dreams would come true…

State of Escape

Different yet the same, she appears again in my dream,
This state of escape is but a strong desire turned real,
                   Perfect to me is she,
                   Perfect to her is me,
The face, the body, the soul, why is she only but a dream?
If only this manifested escape by desire would manifest a
    state which was real.

Day Dream

I just sit here observing people when suddenly I am struck,
Oh perfect ice blue strawberry blonde,
Unaware of her own beauty, she sways as she glides by,
My eyes are fixed upon her consumed by her aura,
She throws a bashful smile my way as she continues on
    out of sight to disappear forever,
Frozen in time I was unable to respond,
Burned into my mind eternally is her image,
(Sigh)…to be in love with a dream is unreal.

My Friend

The Lord says your time here is done,
You've lived your life fulfilling your purpose,
While loving and teaching to love, life's trials you did endure,
Your influence imposed was great,
He now surrounds you with your reward.

> Though I was not, you treated me as one of
>   your own,
> You embraced me as a part of your family.
> You were always there with advice,
> You were always there with a shoulder,
> You were always kind,
> You were always understanding,
> You were always helpful,
> You were always compassionate,
> You were always giving,
> Your love was always touching.

We grieve your passing for ourselves, understanding our
    loss, yet we are grateful your suffering is final,
I hold my arms out wide, letting your spirit pass through
    me, giving you my love and thanking you forever.

Until we meet again,
Goodbye, my friend.

Nightmares

Waking up shaking in the middle of the night,
Falling forever, it seems the most dreadful fright.
Meeting with people who have been dead for two years,
Questioning others who disappear in mirrors.
Sweating profusely as demons enter to fight,
Calling on Christ and praying He makes thing's alright.
Running and yelling, screaming as loud as you can,
Nobody can hear you as you're chased by this man.
Lined up in a row then being shot one by one,
The last one to go I was glad that one was done.
Tired and scared but too tired to stay awake,
Asleep I go again, that chance I'll have to take.

To Ye Who Live to Carry On

To ye who live to carry on, to those who've gone before,
A nod to all, both living and dead, all whom I adored,
For those of you who knew me, and those of you who didn't,
You've all been changed by fate this day, it was no accident!

I have moved on in spirit, my body is in the ground,
Please make a joyful noise for me, and gather all around,
Before I go, pick up a mirror and do this thing for me,
Stare at your face and look real hard and tell me what you see,
I'm in your eyes, I'm in your nose, your mouth is made
     as mine,
I'm in your ears; I'm in your toes, and always in your mind,
Don't mourn for me, I say, *Please don't*, 'cuz part of me
     was you,
And all of me, in return, is forever part of you!

To tell you this I wish I had before I had passed on,
My time has come and I'm not scared, one day we all
     move on,
My life was full and rich, it was, with children all around,
First young, then old, then young again, forever making
     sound,
My elders helped me get a start in life when I was young,
They too moved on while leaving me to carry on their song,
So now I leave to you this note and hope it's not too much,
To everyone who was involved, I loved you a whole bunch!

This is new…I made *me* cry, that hasn't happened fore,
So take a break and wipe *your* eyes, for I have got much
     more…

The Captain of the Poets called, and said *Ye poets write!*
Not that *I* was a *poet*, but I put my pen to flight,
Fond was he of life itself as with *all* its mysteries,
So fond he was he wrote a book of people, wars, and trees,
His fondness so, inspired my soul, it learned how to live,
If only I could touch *yours* too, from death, life's fondness
      give,
How great, I say, it would to be, if all thought life precious,
But then again, would be to write, nothing there'd been
      for us.

So ye who live to carry on, next this I ask of you,
Leave behind your race with rats; stare in to the sky so blue,
Then look below to leaves of grass, the dew upon their blades,
And feel the wind that's moving on, that brushes on your
      face.

Across the field, to trees and such, or down the city street,
See what you see then see some more, then move upon
      your feet,
Find something you've not seen before and look at it real
      close,
You might just find the something that you seem to miss
      the most,
Look in the sky, look in the ground, look in the riverbed,
Search through the trees, search through the weeds, then
      search throughout your head.

The clouds, the crack, the flash that was, little of nature's
      might,
All come about inside your head, confusing more the fight,
The storm, it does, it rages on, nontiring it seems,

When in the end all clear it is, across the sky, sun beams,

Look to the hills, look to the ground, and again gaze to the sky,

New perspective you will have found, when all is wet not dry,

Grass and trees and dogs and things all glitter when weighed with drops,

And life it gives to everything; bugs, birds, and weeds and crops,

Smell the smells, see the sights, hear all the sound that nature makes,

For one day soon, more than you know, of your life they will wake,

Enjoy the life that earth has yet, to give to all of you,

Yea to thee I say *live life!* So the song you leave's on cue.

One last request I make all ye, who live to carry on,

This day, I say, from nature take, before too far you've gone,

Search for you a stone…hold it tight…recall one memory,

Then study its face…take it home…a gift for you from me.

Now as I go, again it's time, to wipe away the tears,

This one last thought I leave for you, to last throughout your years,

The earth, that's life, that once I was, to you is all around,

Again I say, *don't mourn for me*, my life comes from the ground,

So with the setting of the sun across the living sea,

To ye who live to carry on, carry on, without me!

Dream-Maker

Lying there asleep,
What is it you see?
You begin to weep,
I hope it isn't me.

A smile is cracked,
The tears have gone away.
You say you are packed,
Ready to leave today.

Next I hear giggling,
Then laughter abounds.
As if someone is tickling,
You squirm all around.

Suddenly you're still,
And the laughter subsides.
The queen of the hill
Still smiles as she rides.

Observing in awe,
Wondering where it will take her.
Now hope above all,
That I am her dream-maker.

Flyin' Low

All night riding down this tired highway
Flyin' low 'cuz this load is already late.
Wishin' I could sleep and do thing's my way
But this trailer is full of mighty hot freight.

"…Get it here by midnight!"
Was the last I heard them say.
Key…string…kite…
A thought, I didn't say.

One a.m. already and a hundred miles to go.
The road to myself, I grab another gear.
Seventy, eighty, ninety, now I'm really flyin' low,
Thinkin' to myself, "I hope the road stays clear."

Destination in sight, now I gotta slow it down.
Brakes smell hot as I jump out.
There's nobody here and I've looked all around.
Hurry up and wait, that's what it's all about.

Three Crosses

Three crosses stand before me
Of which one was borne for me.
Of the three I should be on one;
All thanks to He who set me free.

No fault of His, the cause was mine,
The cross He bore was for my crime
Of lack of virtue. He on one
Gave His life, in hopes of saving mine.

Three crosses stand before me
Bearing life eternally.
Of the three, I'm not on one;
Praise to He who set me free!
(Baton Rouge, La, north side of I-10)

This Man Sent to Save

I know this Man maybe you know Him too,
Said He came into this world to save me and you,
The Creator's only Son He's the gift that God gave,
And Jesus is the Name of this Man sent to save!

Born in a stable in a manger He lay,
Still performing miracles to this very day,
They called Him a thief yet nothing He stole,
Then they nailed Him to a tree and He saved my soul!

Next they put Him in a tomb 'cuz they thought He was dead,
But little did they know His death was just in their head,
'Cuz three days later… yes this is a fact,
With keys in His hand He came a roaring back!

Now not everyone believes that He is raised,
But my opinion is He's the One to be praised!
With Angels by His side as He went to Heaven,
He said, "For you my child I'll be back again!"
Jesus is the Name of this Man sent to save!

Unknown Love

Though we had met the other week,
We were still unsure just what to speak.
We'd listen to music and with it sing,
But through the hours not say a thing.
We'd be seated and then walk around
All the while being silent through town.
To the park and to the show,
Not to interrupt the flow.

Too very quiet until that last day
When she came to me with these words to say.
"I'm sorry, but I've got to go,
Please listen to the radio.
Tomorrow morning I'll be on
To tell about you to everyone."
I sat there on the ground in awe
Then got up to go tell my Ma.
Before I could leave the park that day,
I had one thing I needed to say,
"I'm sorry but this isn't right,
We haven't had a single fight.
I think we should go our separate ways
And hope to meet up again someday."
She said, "Ok," and that was that.
We said "goodbye" and I put on my hat.

That very next morning, like she said,
I turned on my radio and lay in bed.
She said that she had loads of fun,
And for her, I was number one.
One more thing she said that day,

It was the last I heard her say,
"The only thing that neither of us knew,
Very shy, the other was too."

Dreaming Again

It's been almost sixteen years since I heard the wind call,
It's time to go, just let yourself fall!
I knew I had heard that voice before,
This time it was different, it was offering more.

I've figured out how to take you to a new place!
How would you like to view earth from outer space?
This time, I didn't have to reply,
I just gave in, I didn't ask why.

This time, there was no train station,
Nor was there any unnecessary oration.
It grabbed a hold of every last bit of me
And we were off to a place so that I could see.

I was unsure of just what to say,
But I did wonder if there'd be another day
To come back up here and look all around.
The wind knows me better than a hound.

It said, *don't worry, as was before I will be back,*
I brought you out this time so words at home you wouldn't
    lack.
I had to quit sightseeing, only for a moment,
Just so I could understand exactly what it meant.

No, the wind didn't have to explain,

When I opened my eyes, it was very plain.
I was shown every corner of the earth,
Every nook and cranny since its birth.

My God, we are an unruly people,
We fight about anything, even God at a steeple.
It's obviously been that way since the very beginning,
You'd think by now we'd have found a new chord to sing.

The wind then had something to say,
There was no way it could wait another day,
This madness, it must come to an end!
The earth I roam, no further can bend!

It's spinning faster now, almost out of control!
There must be a new course; you must set a new goal!
It obviously knew that I thought we were striving for peace,
With your brand of peace, my earth must find a new lease!

Again, as then, I found myself in awe,
The world itself would have to come under one law.
Suspended in space, wondering if "one law" should happen,
It said, *if it doesn't, then that place will end.*

Straining my eyes for something different to see,
It brought me up there to view war, not to see glee.
I've given you enough now to ponder,
I must now take those clouds over yonder.

With that, again I was falling,
I strained my ears to hear the wind calling,
Hoping it would come back again to take me away
I found myself in bed waking up to start a new day.

My Dad

Provider, protector, teacher, disciplinarian, foe, guide, friend.
The time came and out into this world, me he did send.
Instinctively providing and always trying to protect,
With values and beliefs my mind he did infect.
Scolded and punished, teaching along the way,
Since I didn't listen, I found trouble every day.
As if my greatest enemy, we'd argue all night long,
Ain't no way I could've been the one who was wrong.
Though I say I didn't listen, I watched every move as well,
Learning to be a man so one day with pride his heart
    would swell.
Continuing to teach when I think I know it all,
He's sharp as a knife, and he's always on the ball.
Though at times he still strives to protect and provide,
My greatest assets from him are that he still mentors and
    guides.
I've grown enough to cherish him until the very end,
For he's more than just my Dad, he's become an awesome
    friend.

Ode to the White Line

Everywhere I connect to this white line,
This white line, everywhere connects to itself,
No distance too great, it's there all the time,
It winds around all over, like one continuous shelf.

At times, it may be hard to see,
It's still there, even when it hides,

Never getting lost, it's just like a bee,
Instinctively all around, it cherishes how it guides.

It connects to Canada, Alaska, and even Mexico,
Like string from Seattle to San Diego, then Bangor and
    Miami,
Tying together all points, be they high or low,
All towns have been united, from "A" to "Z".

It is a warning for the casual traveler,
It cries *stay on my left side, there's danger on my right*!
It is a friend to the weary freight deliverer,
Hypnotizing its patrons as they drive through the night.

It gets run over and scraped and sometimes it fades,
Striving to protect, it's scarred when unsuccessful,
Seldom acknowledged or recognized, its dues have all
    been paid,
Working in every state (on both right sides of the road)
    its resume is full.

Significantly Blind

We are like shrimp at the bottom of the ocean,
Microscopic to the creatures of the universe,
We think we're so great yet what have we done,
So significantly blind, ourselves we still curse.

Looking upward at night through the pinholes in the sky,
Like a cricket in a child's hand not wanting to be contained,

We reach and we gasp, and we jump by and by,
Never realizing we're trapped in a world full of pain.

A predator is near but like sheep we are dumb,
Blind to ourselves our instincts have fled,
To treacherous surroundings, we have turned numb,
A whale glides by, swoosh, we are dead.

True Lost Love

To have her fall in love with me
Was an unbelievable thing to be.
Everything is all that did encompass her
And my young prideful self was what I had to offer.
I worked and I worked and yet I continued to try
Because my side is where I wanted her to be by.

My heart is so filled with pain
My mind at it holds disdain.
To finally let go and allow again to love
Is a gift I've been seeking from High Above.
Though time has passed, over her I can't get,
Ago of her I wish my heart would only let.

Youthful and beautiful she fulfilled a dream,
With, *I love you* from her lips, complete I did seem.
Around our love a home we began to build,
To no one else would our hearts even think to yield.
The love I held for her within would grow more each day,
Shining brighter every moment, just like the morning
    sun's ray.

The pains not as bad as it's been in the past
But longing for her, how long will that last?
I wish it would all just go away
So my second true love could come in some day.
My heart still breaks, by her hands it tore in two,
To offer another love is something right now I can't do.

Oh how I wish I could go back in the past
So I could fix this love which didn't last.
I'd shower her with attention even after a few years
And drown her in affection so her eyes would shed no tears.
I'd love her then as much as I realize I now did
So another man on her heart could not have made a bid.
If only now the pain would subside,
She's got a new life; her love for me has died.
My heart in pieces, it's still scattered all around,
It's been stepped on and kicked and buried in the ground.
To find it all and put back together I hope that I can,
With lessons learned, I long for true love once again.

Peace is Justice

Peace is Justice; Justice is Peace.
Both must derive from within the individual,
Both must be given from one to another,
Both must encompass leaders and be passed on to followers,
Both must govern state and enlighten the world.

At present, states differ in Opinion,
Individuals do as well,
Opinion gets confused for Knowledge and interferes
    with Peace,

Knowledge is gained only from seeking Truth,
Truth in turn is Justice which is equal to Peace.
Peace is Justice; Justice is Peace.

Ghosts

Do you believe in the existence of ghosts?
With no explanation for, I have seen shadows, heard voices,
    and seen what appear to be spirits.
A very physical and binding confrontation in dreams with
    one particular shadow, not a hallucination for others
    saw as well.
Voice out of nowhere, unrecognizable to myself and another.
Figures appearing only to vanish into thin air.
Cold rooms, slamming doors, objects moving that shouldn't,
Appearing to run over people and animals without a trace
    of having hit them.
Feeling as if every move is watched when all alone.
Religious symbols and Bibles not where they were placed,
    never to be found again.
Dogs with uncontrollable fear hoping only to be comforted.
Waking up with someone who's not there staring at you.
Shadows watching from the window while all are in the
    yard, all can see them.
One acts as a protector while the other has motives which
    are undisclosed,
Yet others seem playful and lost to reality.
Call me crazy if you think that you must,
For those who see, I know you're not.
I believe.

A Monkey on the Back

A monkey on the back of a man walking down the road,
Many stories about that sight I saw have been told,
The middle of the city, I just had to laugh,
Metaphor no more, a real monkey this man did have.

Some sayings may be better left unseen,
Like with *the fan* and *a shingle*, you know what I mean,
But this verbal reality now coming to light,
Twinkled like the stars on a clear night.

Queer and goofy it made me smile,
At least the monkey on my back won't leave a pile,
For that one moment in time I was not alone,
'Cuz this man and his monkey down the street did roam.

The monkey on my back may be invisible to the rest,
Weighing me down it is quite the pest,
A new home for this animal would be great to find,
To finally get it off my back and out of my mind.

During moments it seems that I am down,
I reflect back on a time going through that town,
Visualizing a monkey weighing down on that man,
Dealing with burdens, I understand that I can.

Greatness

Is there anything left that's great for us?
Dickenson, Faulkner, Poe, and Whitman,
Mathew, Mark, Luke, and John,
Shakespeare, Plato, Aristotle, and Homer,
A few who set literary standard so high.

Lewis and Clark and Sam Houston,
Christopher Columbus and Magellan,
Setting out to discover new worlds,
Unknowingly planting seeds for societies.

Trains and cars and cities and towns,
Skyscrapers, tunnels, bridges, and dams,
Putting man in the air and then into space,
Mans conquered a lot, these things have been great.

What's next? I say I must have to ask,
Greatness it seems is a difficult task,
Have all the great things already been done,
Have we been left in awe, by historical man?

They learned navigation on both land and sea,
Gold and silver they dug up in glee,
Theology and philosophy they set us on a course,
We're stuck still trying to perfect their ideas.

With stories and NEWS and poetry that stays,
Their greatness has lasted more than their day,
I wonder if they knew the things that they did,
Would last this long and great by us be viewed.

That gives me hope that there is still greatness left to be
     achieved,
For I seriously doubt their greatness they'd ever believe,
One day, maybe, long after we're gone,
Popular opinion could be that great, of us was one.

War

Righteousness made this country great,
Greatness has not, however, made this country always right.
Politicians, for example, are not always right.
When they think they are, it is only a matter of their own
     opinion,
They call their opinion knowledge and assume that it is truth.
Opinions are unique to individuals, therefore they cannot
     agree,
Compromise is unattainable, for individually they think
     they are right.
Opinion is not knowledge, it is merely a belief based on
     a probability.
Knowledge, however, is truth.
Truth is proven and constant, opinion varies.
With truth constant, there is only one truth,
Hence, there is only one knowledge.
With only one true knowledge, there cannot be opinion,
Without opinion, there cannot be war.
When the world finds truth it will be knowledgeable,
When knowledgeable, conflict will not be possible, war
     will not survive.

My Dear

I wait for her, my first born; realizing the error of my ways.
Is she ever going to wish to know who I am?
Will she ever care that I'm still alive?
Has she been told about me and ever wondered where I was?
Does she even wonder about me at all and what it would
    be like if I were there?
If she has been told, what sort of things has her mother,
    uncle, brother, grandparents, and friends had to say?
    Not certain any of them could be kind.
Will I ever be able to be a part of her life?
If I was to say to her, *I thought about you every day and still
    do*, would she even consider that to be true?
Does she hate me now and will she forever?
Surely she couldn't believe me if I claimed my love for her
    was strong, could she? That would have to be hard for
    her to comprehend, for that I have never proven.

I wonder what she likes and what not; I wonder how she's
    growing,
I wonder what she knows; I wonder how she thinks,
I wonder if she's stubborn and strong; I wonder if she's
    the leader of her friends or someone who just goes
    along; I wonder if she's shy,
I wonder if she's compassionate and caring; I wonder if
    she's disheartened and cold,
I wonder what she wants to be when she grows up; I
    wonder in what areas she excels and enjoys in school,
I wonder what grade she's in; I wonder if she deems it
    important,

I wonder if she believes in God; I wonder if she has faith in people,

I wonder if she cries at night; my heart breaks at the thought,

I wonder about her sense of humor; I wonder what things are considered to be serious by her at this stage,

I wonder what foods are her favorites; I wonder which one's she can't stand,

I wonder what she's fond of on TV; I wonder what movies she adores,

I wonder who her favorite musicians are; I wonder if she's anything like me,

I wonder how she feels inside her mind; I wonder what questions she now expels,

I wonder if she has long hair or short; I wonder what shade it is,

I wonder if I would recognize her if I were to see; I am certain she is beautiful!

I wonder what portions, if any of this, I will ever know,

I wonder what answers to her I will ever be able to provide; can any of them even be sufficient? Will I even be given or ever take that chance? Only time holds that answer, for shame and fear control me.

I long to have hugs and kisses from her,

To hold her close,

To tickle her and hear her laugh,

To share in all the little insignificant things which somehow never are; that would be awesome,

To share affection, thoughts, time; this I most desire,

To kiss her *owies* making her better and tuck her in at night chasing monsters from her room,

To watch her sleep and be there when she awakens,

To listen to her breathe,

To laugh with her when she burps; to leave the room when it comes out the other end,

To bless her when she sneezes,

To comfort her when she cries,

To calm her when she's frightened,

To care for her when she's ill,

To listen to her heart beat,

To watch her play,

To watch her run,

To see her fall down so I may pick her up and brush her off and send her on her way,

To make her breakfast, lunch, and dinner observing the faces she makes when she tastes something not appealing to her tongue,

To notice her interaction with animals and people, or lack thereof,

To show her for the first time, cities, mountains, waterfalls, canyons, deserts, wildlife, lakes, oceans, forests; The Creators imagination,

To see the awe in her face at Disneyland, meeting Minnie and Mickey, Donald, Goofey, Cinderella, Snow White and more; to see the amazement in her eyes at the fireworks before we leave,

To see her reaction to something funny or sad,

To see the compassion in her eyes for victims of disaster,

To watch her grow,

To watch and help her learn,

To train her in her thoughts,

To answer her questions, even if I don't know the answer,

To teach her about the essence of life; we could learn
    together, for I too am still learning,
To encourage her in the endeavors of her choice,
To give her a sense of security and trust; that may never
    be achieved by me,
To just look into her eyes and connect to her soul; quite
    possibly the completion of my own,
To absorb the joy on her face on her birthday or at
    Christmas; I've missed it all,
I long just to know her and for her forgiveness; will these
    I ever know?

E. A. P. (Love's Burden)

The burden of his love he bore
In rhyme and rhythm of English lore,
A lieutenant of prose [to make a living],
A man whose learning's were far and near –
A brokenness inside – from love to fear –
A bard's – however – is the life he chose.
To be remembered was all he wished –
(Sickness from love – all to blame),
"The Raven" of course is what made his fame –
To be a Poet, was his lifetime wish.
From one who claimed "no poem is long" –
He cried big tears in every song.

When death broke his heart no more
He then became the Sergeant Major.

Turning

Heartache pains wholly my soul
As time's destiny onwardly tolls
Towards destiny's place in time;
War fills space like rhyme –
Poverty submissively chimes –
Arrogance presides sublime.

Onward world turn –
Turn, churn, and turn
Without sense for more – turn –
And find destiny's place in time!
Forget me as I observe,
Not having a chance to make less absurd
The goals of men – not bird –
While in search for destiny's place in time.

Turn world! Turn –
Turn, churn and burn
Through space – for peace – we yearn
As destiny's place in time!

(No Title)

It's 4 a.m. again,
My mind's indulged the same,
In verse of yesterday.

I've heard the voice of Frost;
I've seen through Whitman's eye;

I've feared the heartache of Poe;
I've lived with Dickenson's immortal soul.
It's 4 a.m. again,
Mind now wanders to find its name,
In verse now for today.

(No Title)

To get to "B" from "A";
How to do that today
With narcissism rampant,
Ignoring non-self constant,
Blind to the boulder around the curve,
Too awful late to swerve –
Collision inevitable,
Crash course – enabled –
"B" is further now than before –
"A" is the only lore.

An Evolving Definition...

The most perfect poetry (in one sense of course)
combines literature, visualization of imagination with
Frost's "imagining ear" in idealizing, in any direction,
what is reality. It ought to "make sense in the day," use
some "book speak," and appear to be a dream (the perfect
experience for mind, at least in reading).
To be continued?

She Smiles

I see her walk across the prairie
Dressed as days gone by,
A child of eight or maybe nine, (or ten, eleven, or twelve,)
She pauses in her strideful path,
Takes time to pick a daisy.
She puts it close up by her mouth
Breathes in her nose and smiles,
Spreads her arms and twirls about
(She spins and spins and spins,)
She stops and falls onto the ground
And rolls and laughs aloud.
Real close she looks at the flowers around
Consoling the ones alone.
Gently touching she whispers to them
What, I am unaware.
She closes her eyes and smells their perfume
And once again she smiles.

Again I see her walk across the prairie
Dressed as days gone by,
A young woman of twenty-eight or nine (grown up no longer
      a child),
She pauses in her busy day,
Takes time to pick a daisy.
She puts it close up by her mouth
Breathes in her nose and smiles,
Spreads her arms and twirls about
(Not spinning as fast this time,)
She stops and helps herself to the ground
And rolls and laughs aloud.

Real close she looks at the flowers around
Consoling the ones still alone.
Gently touching she whispers to them
A few more words this time.
She closes her eyes and absorbs their perfume,
And once again she smiles.

Once more I see her walk across the prairie
Dressed as days gone by,
An elderly lady of, I assume eighty-nine, (grown up and
    now full lived),
With her day no longer busy she's come out to gaze around
And takes time to pick a daisy.
She puts it close up by her mouth
Breathes in her nose and smiles,
She spreads her arms and stares to the sky,
(No longer venturing to twirl about),
She gently collapses to the ground
And gives her last sigh aloud.
Real close the flowers now look at her
Consoling the one alone,
Gently touching they weep for her,
Her words to them were alive.
They close her eyes and bathe her with perfume,
And one last time she smiles.

Duties

I don't really want to go
But I really think I ought to though.
She says she really needs to pee
But it's rainy and snowy and cold you see.

By herself I'd let her go
To run and play in the snow.
From the leash I'd set her free,
But then I know she wouldn't pee.

She's not the type that'll just come back,
She sniffs and runs and has to ransack.
Until she's all worn out she won't come back to me,
And then she's still got to go pee.

I'll put on my coat and that goofy hat,
And hope she won't see a cat,
And I'll take her out 'til her bladder is free,
And she can leave a puddle of pee!

(It's gonna be cold and I don't like that
So I put on my coat and that silly hat.
By now she's at my feet you see,
She's really got to pee!)

Patriotism

Patriotism in America is dead.
That's right; you heard what I said,
It's dead.

Assimilation has become a bore,
From a million to one no longer the score,
Now one to many and many more,
Assimilation is no more.

Heritage, of course, should be retained
To remember from which where we came,
But a culture of one should be gained;
Our history and domination should not be shamed.

For forty years now, dying has become its fame.
Politicians out of patriotism have made a game
And higher education has defamed its name,
This country may never again be the same!

Heroes such as Washington and Lincoln have faded away,
And Columbus, now no one celebrates his day.
The tea party at Boston in the Bay
Has been tarred and feathered I dare to say.
We ended slavery and discrimination.
We opened freedom to every nation.
We fought hard wars and them we won,
They were not pretty; in blood countless tons.

Now history has changed and our efforts were wrong.
For a world without *US* it seems some long,
Within our borders they are very strong,
Denouncing patriotism is their song.

Have they succeeded while we lay in bed?
Is patriotism in America truly dead?
Will we believe what these voices have said
And accept for real that patriotism is dead?

Has patriotism become a bad word?
It's batted around as if it's something absurd,
Careless use has altered the meaning of this word,

And offense taken without its questioning inferred,
Now that is what is absurd!

It derives from the history of ONE nation,
A common God and a superior religion,
Common law indiscriminate to none,
A society inferior to not one.

History as it was must be taught!
True understanding from the past must be caught
In the minds of our young should a strong future be sought
With a nation above all others as for which its past fought.

Again I dare and suggest it still breathes
But we must rise as ONE before it leaves
Or of a nation our children will soon grieve,
As patriotism drowned and flowed off our sleeves.

Necessity for a nation; it must be bred.
Patriotism in America as yet is not dead!
That's right; I hope some have heard what I've said
To prohibit patriotism in our land from becoming dead.
(I pray this thought is all in my head
And patriotism in America's not dying to dead!)

Boyhood Dream

Men dream of boyhood things.
Up on the stage she sings
Of days gone by (the woman too dreams).
For the girl of then he longs it seems
Before years morphed each to now.

Winter's Flurry

Maybe I ought to change my way of thinking
And send my thought back to new in spring;
Blossoms are vivid all around now
With new life finding way somehow,
Carefully surviving the storms to maturity it vows.

On through fall appearing to die
To dormancy next as winter lies;
Again the rain before life springing
With flying residents returned gaily singing
To forge through war which nature brings.

Each generation clings to new life
Severing the last as with a knife;
Pushing through new growth its past did buy,
Enduring the storms to winter to lie
Dormant again waiting for spring as old dies.

Cycles continue to move on.
New takes over as the old becomes gone.
Leaves again green new life reaching for sun,
Hoping to grow tall before their day is done
To become with the stars none less than one.

It's gonna happen; nothing I can do
Except recline and observe nature's natural zoo.
Ah, it'd be nice to relax without worry
When my generation gets in a hurry
To change the landscape before winter's flurry.

Wild Fire

It rages across the field so mean,
It devastates all as it cleans,
It even jumps across the stream,
The race is on it seems.
Up the hill and down the next,
Upon the land its print is text,
It rises where the brush collects,
It slides across where roads intersect.
It's pushed by wind
It's fed by land
It drives away even modern man;
It burns because it can.

This Path

My claim to know; is it such a gem?
Am I just as self-righteous then as them?
Equality has become that all thought's the same,
No one is better; isn't that insane?
A world where reality is different to each,
Elimination of common goals for which to reach,
Dispersing community and human bonds,
Erasing the history making Nationalism gone.
This path, it seems, has been started down,
Has it reached near to you yet in your town?

I Write

To understand my own mind
Releasing thoughts from a space confined,
I write.
Inside sometimes completely confused,
My mind it seems is a bit obtuse,
A vision of thought is the way I observe,
To accept ideas as normal or completely absurd,
I write.
Watching my thought as it lands on the page,
A wandering beast no longer caged,
Creating a new realm in which mind now can engage
To act out its play upon a wider stage,
I write.

Searching

Searching for love I find her,
Never away far, she remains there,
I found her again and again
The way I always have (since I was ten).
Her existence is real it has been since,
It just always had not made sense.
Locked away at times hidden from me
I open my heart and I can see
That she is here with me.

Searching for love I find her.
Away in body a different connection is there.

Souls travel in ways unknown
Through time and space it seems they roam
To their match; themselves in perfect time
They carry on a distant rhyme,
Love for her has never gone
I open my heart as if it were dawn
To see two souls as one.

Searching for love I find her.
Always within; she's there.

Perfectly Still

I write to forget my present time,
I write to try and reset my mind,
I try to forget the memories I find,
I stare blankly out into the night,
The trees are perfectly still.

Moths and June bugs fly around the light,
Fluorescents flicker before losing sight,
Nature now seems perfect and right,
I sit in darkness thoughtlessly blind,
The trees are perfectly still.

I try to write but I cannot see
The things beyond; so black are thee,
With only the dark out there for me
I rest my pen and drift off to dream,
The trees are perfectly still.

Neglecting to Go

Time to leave mind behind,
Memories only tend to bind,
Making the day surrounding blind
From love and life and current mind.

Life abounds around today,
With mind lost, stashed away,
Locked in time from yesterday,
Watching now pass as it lay.

Beauty and passion overlooked now
Not recognized though all around somehow,
Yesterday seen today is low
With mind stuck in time passed neglecting to go.

Always Sad

Always sad is a miserable way,
This way she is, she told me today.
I don't know why, she didn't say that,
Only that's how she is and that was that.

I know how she feels for I am too,
Life never works out it just happens for me and you.
Looking back, envisioning my now from when I was a child,
The vision seen then is not the one that was dialed.

Those dreams I still carry, they're still in my mind,
Getting lost in those memories, those dreams I can find,

But more than that, they are no more,
Just guarded dreams by a broken door.

Always sad is a miserable way,
This way she is, she told me today.
One lone thing that would make me glad,
Would be if she wasn't always sad!

More Than One

Heartache caused by more than one,
Three bricks collide, each weight a ton.
First a crack, a broken line,
Visible enough though it was fine.
Second it broke; it tore in two,
Pain inside from number two.
Third one crushed; scattered the pieces around,
Final destruction without a sound.

Heartache caused by more than one,
Three bricks collide, each weight a ton.
The day it cracked, it had begun,
Permanent damage though it was young.
Then it broke; the beginning of the end,
A hand, the soul no longer could lend.
Older and stronger, still the last blow did crush,
Silencing its beat to a lonesome hush.

Heartache caused by more than one,
Three bricks collide, each weight a ton.
First one significant inside the mind,

Second today, is still blind,
Three was catcher of all the wrath,
These three broke one along their path.
Not one but all three broke this heart,
They each at their time performed their part.

One Week in July

I fell in love when I was young,
For her my heart beat like a drum,
As we grew older that love was still there,
A week in July we were able to share,
Back to our lives we had to go,
Below the bottom my heart sank low,
I've written and thought about her all my life,
Wishing I'd had that chance to make her my wife,
Love for her has stayed in my heart,
Doing little except tear me apart.
My mind goes through a wringer but falls down into
    its puddle only to absorb it all again and repeat this
    hellish process.

She's not to blame, she loved me too,
Control was not ours; there was nothing for us to do,
We were kids; we had to play their game,
Not knowing our hearts would never be the same,
Like Romeo and Juliet our hearts were one,
For the same reason as them, our happiness was gone,
We've moved on with life getting to where we are now,
Only to wish for a time we could go back to somehow,
Knowing the probability for that is less than real,

We suck up our dreams, continue to love, and pray our
    hearts will heal.

If we could only have that one week in July, every week
    for the rest of our lives, we would be complete.
(Both of our hearts were broken before we were old
    enough to understand by those who had the least
    right to do so)

Cheated and Torn

She came to me in my dream distraught and broken,
Her dream again the same as it was back then,
Perfection in love the object of her quest,
Dissatisfaction with life seemed normal at best,
Cheated and torn is how life left her feel,
Still in search of her dream and love so real.

Who am I

A question posed to me, divided,
How did the military change you and who you are?
Not sure how the military changed me but it probably did.
Without being on separate paths simultaneously, not sure
    I will ever know.

Revising the second part, *Who am I?* Huh, what a question,
Not sure I know completely, but I will try…

I am just a man who tries to be just, not certain there is anything special, different, or complicated about me,

I am a product of my culture, from it my opinions have been formed and knowledge gained; I disagree with about half of my society, if not more,

I am a son, loyal yet bitter at times about my youth,

I am a dad who will do anything helpful for my children (and other children); thankful the Lord gave us the opportunity to borrow them from Him, for they are really His,

I am an ex-husband, twice,

I am a friend to anyone who needs one; bums, homeless, strangers, family, acquaintances, and people I've known "forever",

I am a man who is quiet and shy,

I am determined,

I am a loner who is lonely,

I am one in search of knowledge,

I am one who hates untruths,

I am one in search of love,

I am one in love with a dream,

I am one who accepts reality but hates it,

I am a man disappointed with life, I feel it has mislead and cheated me,

I am a man in love with someone I cannot have,

I am a man, a man with a broken heart,

I am a worker bee in a society without a queen,

I, am well traveled,

I am lost and broken and confused and hurt,

I am a wanderer without a home; a house does not count,

I am a man who is withdrawn,

I am almost content but not happy; I long to be happy,

I am disgusted by the way I was lied to as a child, I could be anything or anyone I wanted because I grew up in America; without a silver spoon that all remains a dream as well; even with hard work in America you are a pawn for society,

I am able to carry on, even when I don't want to,

I am a strong man in the face of adversity,

I am a man filled with emotions which cannot escape my head but sometimes try, only to return to hibernation once again,

I am one who strives to be moral,

I am opinionated,

I am mournful,

I am prideful,

I am a sinful man,

I am shameful,

I am a man distraught by decisions made along my journey, by myself and others,

I am a man discouraged by the world, somewhat pessimistic about its future while trying to remain optimistic,

I am a man who believes The Prophets,

I can be confrontational when nerves are struck, yet mostly I am calm,

I, am a writer – doesn't matter if I'm a good one or not – I am a writer,

I am a man who enjoys music; both to listen to and sing,

I am a man who lives inside my past most of the time since the present isn't always appealing,

I am in search of a pleasant future,

I am a man, who runs as fast as he can from reality in pursuit of a dream,

This is who I am, for now.

Pen to Paper

Putting pen to paper, not sure what will come out,
Knowing something will be in the end, there is no doubt,
My hand slides across the paper,
My fingers guide, and ink appears.

What will they say, I don't really know,
I'll read it when they're done, the writing will show,
My mind goes blank and I gaze off far away,
Turn my pen loose; for still, it cannot stay.

It dances gracefully across the page,
Words come out from inside its cage,
It tells the world what's in my mind,
It has the ability for words to find.

Without this pen I would be lost,
For with being shy there comes a cost,
Without this release, within it would remain,
My head would explode, or at least be insane.

I Was Asked

I was asked if I remembered when…
I haven't replied as yet, but yes, I remember a lot of when.
Reflecting on people is something I have a lot of time for,
Remembering those I love and those times I still long for.
Catching me by surprise, a question by someone in my
    past clear out of the blue,

From a time I'd put long away and moved on from, two
    lifetimes ago came back from out of the blue.
I figured she had forgot about a time really not so long ago,
When singing about forever and how together through
    life we'd go.
Thinking and writing about the longest love from my past,
Always remembering when, before time made then pass.
(Yes Kimi, I will always remember when…)

Universal Quest

Sometimes I wonder about withering away,
As if to another realm.
It seems at times I'm already there,
Invisible to my surroundings.
Stares go through me incapable of being real,
Just peer right passed me unrecognizable to the minds.

If I did just wither away my cares would all abandon,
No worry about health, or life, or limb; carefree in some
    other dimension.
I'd float around from here to there visiting all different times,
I'd leave this world to venture on and marvel at my finds.
The clouds, the moon, the planets and stars are waiting
    for my arrival,
The concerns of life back here on earth no longer would
    be vital.
I'd pour the rain and place the stars; slide down the
    Milky Way,
Spin Saturn then sling the stars, while surfing the sun's
    gold ray.

Black holes would be my playground, shooting through
    them all,
Bending space to warp all time would soon become my call.
I'd skip from here to there unknown oblivious to time,
I'd search the universe for its walls; of which I'd never find.
I'd roam and roam and roam some more for all eternity,
I'd quest for love and truth and God; the same reality.

As if cold water splashed my face, I return again to here,
My shape is back and me now all seem to recognize,
No longer unseen I look around and this space I observe,
I am a part of something here that's common to us all;
A desire by all to be perceived as real, and a universal
    quest for love and truth and God.

Two Young Lovers'

If only we as two young lovers'
Had listened to the poets and seized the day
We would not be unhappy with our others;
Looking back to then for love such as they.

Present is sometimes too full to notice;
The past is much easier to see,
The passing moment from which is passed a kiss
Becomes most precious later, as a memory.

"Carpe Diem" are the words of Frost
About two in love lost to the day.
Off to where he did not know
Afraid that of their love themselves were lost.

It sounds like us when we were young;
Carefree and laughing and carrying on,
Oblivious to the love we shared;
It took then to pass to see we cared.
It can be confusing with now entangled
With aspects of our lives surrounding
The true love before us as it dangles
Amidst the chaos in life abounding.

Seize the day young lovers'!
Forget the noise of others.
Be happy with the love you share
For love like yours is rare.

Everlasting Rose

Her aroma still catches in me from across the room,
The petals are vivid which created her perfume.
I caught a glimpse of the rose when she walked by
Her existence a vision captured which fore to now lie
In mind everlasting; even after I die.

Meaning, Love

A glimpse of yesterday came through her smile;
A memory recognizable by her laugh.
Through her eyes the past traveled many miles
Completely through to today; the way did not stop at half.

What is it I search for away from fear?
Meaning, love? They seem not near.
Lightning flashes in many ways
Chasing the past right into today.

Purpose is void sometimes it seems.
(The sparkle in her eye now gleams.)
Fulfillment in love was lost to the past
For fear that new could never last.
She smiles and laughs and even giggles again,
(I wonder where she's been.)
Reality bites as time catches up,
Handing me again an empty cup.

Her smile is pretty; her laugh I just love;
She breathes perfume from above.
Diamonds in her eyes as she looks away,
Meaning, love? Probably not real today.

Poets Inquire

Poets inquire of life and death,
Of love and hate and soul and mind
With only their own in hopes to find
Before they sigh their last breath.

The quest, or claim, to understand
Is what exudes from each their hands
No matter from which they claim their land
They continue turning over the glass of sand
And question the same as the ones before
Or declare their minds are filled with more
And espouse with conviction their lore.

From religion to science to politics we hum,
A piece of culture we have become
But nature and love are our favorite songs
Before death brings the knowledge for which we long.

Poets inquire of obvious existence
Desiring to know all before mortality
To understand the next reality
This one prepares us for hence.

The Meadow

My mind takes me to a place I've never been,

There are lilacs and daisies, oaks, willows, and firs,

A narrow stream with clear running water leading into
a pond,

Lilly pads and reeds, tad poles, minnows, and largemouth
bass,

One mountain reaching skyward appears at the end of
the water, strange, it seems not to belong,

I turn and the stream turns with me, now the pond feeds it,

It calls me to follow it across the meadow; I walk silently
with the stream,

I stare out across the open meadow and behold, a lone
fawn shows its face,

Without fear its steps are leading towards me, it walks
through me to the stream and disappears,

The stream continues to call me and I obediently follow,

There are rabbits and squirrels, prairie dogs and raccoons,
all seemingly unaware of anything besides the stream;
it calls them too, as with the fawn, they too disappear,

I am more curious by each scene provided, the streams
allurement now binds me; I continue on,

The sky is so clear and blue it almost blinds, the sun is
not visible but it must be high,

Three eagles appear, one is golden, one is small, and
dynamic the one which is bald,

They circle closely then two land, one on my right arm
another on my left, the bald tempted too much dives
into the stream; the others soon follow,

Now effortlessly, as if a stream of my own, I continue
through the meadow,

Glancing back to see where I've been, the mountains gone, the ponds gone, the sky's gone, the stream does not exist behind me; as if history itself has died,

Facing forward again I realize I am now one with the stream, no longer does it call me, it surrounds me,

A wolf stands alone on the boulder just watching the stream as I go by; I did not turn to see its fate for I know it no longer survives,

I move faster now, as if time is speeding up,

All creation now throws itself into the water; I wince, everything becomes a blur,

Faster, faster, yet faster I move; the fear subsides as soon as it arrives, the stream now comforts,

I fall…

There is nothing to see, there is nothing to grasp, it appears there is nothing at all,

Still, I am falling…still…

My fall has ended; I am on the bottom looking up,

Where is the sky, where is the land, where are the trees, flowers, and creatures,

I look around, nothing is clear, the noise is deafening, the roar…it won't go away,

Panic sets in; I can't breathe and realize I should,

I move, there is resistance, the stream is gone, bubbles appear,

The fall…waterfall! I must swim with the air of life and find the surface,

Legs and arms are weak; I force them to work,

The darkness begins to go away, I still do not see the surface; I kick harder,

How much further? I am tired; I can't make it…

I awaken in a meadow,

My mind takes me to a place I've never been,

There are lilacs and daisies…

Ripping Apart

Ripping apart from inside out
A thorn in the side there is no doubt
Constantly wondering when it will end
Forever chasing one's mind around their head
The feeling encompasses the body whole
It makes one ill inside their skull
Sleep it deprives through night and day
Consuming all energy which had been saved
Invoking thought and fear alike
Through one's body it does hike
Even when the cause is known
It won't go away it continues to grow
The fear it creates can make one insane
To look at life again never the same
Accomplishment or time may be solutions
For the body anxiety is this pollution

It churns stomachs it weakens knees
Turns arms to jelly on minds it bleeds
Diverting thoughts and necessary chores
Closing the mind to opportunistic doors
Try to suppress it to no avail
For this crime there is no bail
The mind and body are its victims
Running rampant anxiety rules them
This villain continues along its course
Taking its toll showing no remorse
Breaking one's will and faith for their future
This beast called anxiety in an awful creature

Listening to Music in the Cold

I saw you the other day at Wal-Mart,
You were focused on stuffing things into your cart,
I just sort of shuffled right on by,
Then memories of you came gushing into my mind.
Trying to get away from them I strived to remember what
    I needed,
But it was no use and to my mind I finally conceded.
My nose then started playing tricks on me,
It was a sweet memory for my nose to see,
I smelled the perfume you always wore,
As if, it seemed, it had overcome the store,
I found myself sitting in a corner surrounded by shoes,
But not before the trips in my mind had been turned loose.

I remembered the days when we first were together,
It seemed at the time that they would last forever,
We'd get a six pack and go park on a dirt road,
We never "did it," just sat there talking, listening to music
    in the cold.
This is a memory that seems to haunt me the most,
Our friendship was strong; we seemed to have been so close,
Other memories kept pouring in and out,
But that is the one which seems to hold clout.

I remembered bowling on a Saturday night,
Skating in the park with you on my right,
Sitting on the bank waiting for a bite,
Then chasing the frogs, oh, you were a sight!

Drinking a beer as we were parked on a dirt road,
Dreaming and talking, listening to music in the cold.
I remembered your long hair, and through it, how my
     fingers would rake,
And how out of nowhere a kiss you would just take,
Then holding hands as we'd stroll around the lake,
And laughing at you when you screamed at that snake.

Drinking a beer as we were parked on a dirt road,
Dreaming and talking, listening to music in the cold.

We went to the show and we went to the mall,
We sat on the couch and we watched football,
When we were apart, the other we'd call,
We were a couple it seemed above all.

No more beer as we were parked on a dirt road,
We held each other dreaming and talking, listening to music
     in the cold.

With those memories from the sight of you now coming
     to light,
It was still of no use, I couldn't remember what I had
     come in for that night,
So I steadied myself and I rose to my feet,
Then walked to my car and drove down the street,
I pulled into a gas station, grabbed a six pack for the road,
Then parked by myself, dreamed and listened to music
     in the cold.

Drinking a beer as I was parked on a dirt road,
Remembering a dream, listening to music in the cold.

This Great Idea

This great idea of America endures by its innovation, agriculture, diverseness, adaptability, technology, industry, government, cities, people, nature, and land.
What an idea and courage its founders had!
What nobleness, pride, and determination its citizens have contained!
What bravery and might its defenders have shown!
What sorrow we feel for the lost in battle, for the benefit of their fight they could not reap.
What openness and compassion our shores allow!
What opportunity this idea continues to provide for the weak, the tired, the poor, the hungry!
From all around they strive to be within her boundaries to continue their struggle less encumbered.
What vastness is emitted throughout its geography so that it can accommodate all kinds!
What life it has given to the rest of the world by invention and shameless transference throughout!
What optimism we have for the future of this land!
This great idea continues to evolve,
Oh America! How wonderful it is to be between your shores!

From the Mouth of a Child

From the mouth of a child nine years complete,
He caught me off guard while driving down the street.
Nowhere from

Did this thought come
But it on my heart did land,
I don't like the word ex-husband!

I don't like the word either,
Ex-wife, second, third, or fourth neither.
A lot of pain these words cause,
Life and sanity is all but lost.
Hate is how he expressed his feeling toward that word,
Believe me when I say his feeling all too well I heard.

Sophisticates

No longer are the sophisticates today sonorous to me,
Soporific is more like what the word should be,
They appear to be like kine, lily-livered as such,
All the while acting as moppets playin' with their lunch.

A linden, now that knows how to rollick,
Sophisticates only know how to fuss and kick,
Better than you they think their 100 times,
For their snobbish air, I'd give not even a dime.

We must all be wise in the ways of the world to some degree,
Necessarily that doesn't mean we should all have to agree,
But those who feel their sophisticated by a greater means,
Have never lived in my world and don't know me.

Thankful...

For children who make me think and hysterically laugh
   out loud.
For parents who allow me to dream and encourage my
   success.
A sister who picks me up when I'm down and can make
   dust a cloud.
For a brother-in-law whom time spent with is nothing
   but the best.

For friends considered as family who keep loneliness at bay,
For other family who act as friends letting me just be me.
A skill which affords opportunity and provides every day.
For a house I call my home where kids grow filling my
   memory.

For air rides cabs and power steering and roads which
   have all been paved.
For all the people and services provided along the way.
A loyal companion named Roxy even when she's not
   behaved.
For Father, Son, and Holy Spirit, lighting the path every day.

This Time

Another winter is here
Which means the end to another year
Snow is already falling
And on Santa the kids are calling.

The sounds of kernels popping
The hustle and bustle and shopping
The quest for the perfect gift
Like grains of sand through the stores we sift
Music and bells a ringing
Every now and then someone singing
Yes, it's Christmas time again
The time when Christ came to save all man.

Religion

To be left untouched by poets,
Not subject of greatness,
Not important to Democracy,
Not pertinent to a societies character,
A rule of *The Captain* – religion not to be subject of poetry
    if one to be poet for America,

I take issue with that and will break *the rule*,

To be greatly poetic one must touch on all that make
    Democracy a real idea,
Religion drives our Democracy,
              We want *freedom of religion*,
              We want *freedom from religion*,
              We acknowledge a Creator,
              We say we are the creators,
              We base laws on religious values,
              Yet want God to not be a part of society,
              Take Him out of the Courts,
              Take Him out of our schools,
              Take Him out of *The Pledge of Allegiance*,

Take Him out of our parks,
Be gone from anything considered "Public
    Property!"
Next step, kick Him out of His own House,
Kick Him out of His own Book!

To each his own…
Religion has been the greatest piece of this Democracy,
Freedom to worship (or not) as each individual sees fit,
Until recently, with no fear of persecution from government,
(People have always persecuted the faithful),

If one understands history, one understands that this
    Democracy was founded because of religion; its base is
    religion,
           Some Founders were Christian,
           Some Founders were atheist,
           Some were otherwise indifferent,
All agreed that God created all man equal with God
    given, not man given, rights.
I say, no harm with God visible in society,
Don't like it, close your eyes, turn your head, don't believe it,
No harm done to you (unless it invokes guilt),
No harm to me.

How have we allowed *political correctness* and *sensitivity
    training* to lead us here?
We allow ourselves to be offended by the one thing
    which has made this country great – FREEDOM to
    practice religion or not.

To those who are offended, GET OVER IT!

Early on this Morn

Early on this morn I pose to you a question:

Since neither theorists can prove their argument to be truth, who do you believe and why?

Maybe that's not exactly the question I have, how about this one:

Between theories of spontaneity and evolution, and creation by a Creator, which do you adhere to?

Let me refine yet a step further:

For ye who say there is no God, if in death you learn God does exist, will it not be too late to elude His wrath?

If those who believe God does exist, and in death learn there is no God, what exactly have they lost?

In my opinion, God must exist, science cannot prove otherwise, hence past and present scientists have come to believe.

There is no other way to explain the simplicity and complexity of the universes, ours and ourselves included, other than saying everything is a "freak of nature."

Everything an accident or coincidence, not likely.

If I am wrong, I have lost nothing, if right; have won the game of life.

Your turn to answer.

There Were Those Who Once Wondered

There were those who once wondered what was on the other side of the sea,

Today we know.

There were those who once wondered what it would be like
 to be in the sky,
Today we know.
There were those who once wondered what the earth would
 look like from outer space,
Today we know.
There were those who once wondered about Mars and
 Saturn,
Today, we are learning.
There are those who are wondering what the future brings
 through new technology, exploration, and man's hand,
Tomorrow, you will know.

Continuing the Completion

To the dreamers of a day gone by
Your dreams by us have been achieved
To those who achieve only what we today may dream
Your dreams will be achieved by those who follow

Wandering

I find my mind out wandering
It wanders all alone,
It cries while it's away from me
For a time which is unknown.

Mind finds my body wandering
It too wanders all alone,
Without emotion, wandering,
Through a time which is unknown.

The Oblivion

Telling Time to just move on
You drift off into oblivion,
Wishing that aspect to leave you alone,
Time moves faster and takes you along,
There's no escaping; you can't make it stop,
Out of its grasp you only wish to drop.

It changes who you are; it starts from the top,
Your mind, then your soul, it plants its own crop,
The colors change, they're not your own,
Showing the signs that those seeds were sown,
Time has a way of continuing on,
The ride with Time is the oblivion.

Three Times She Cried

Three times she cried I remember well,
The first time to she, what did he tell?
The next a situation which wasn't right,
She cried for days, many a sleepless night.
The third was the time to her I gave a name,
Still haunting my soul and filling with shame.
I wish that she had never cried
And had had a place from all this to hide,
It was long ago yet for the time(s) by me,
I beg for forgiveness; I forever am sorry.

Gone For Now

Gone for now are the demons within,
They've been put in their place; I showed them somehow,
Locked away they've been put in their tin,
Back home is my heart and I'm happy for now.

Having more control than I once thought,
I booted them out and made room for my heart,
Surfing through time my heart again caught,
The past fin'ly let go, from me it did part.

Understanding I'm free to move on,
Now I can deal with what the past left for me,
While knowing with morning will come dawn,
Again a tomorrow to set myself free.

Time

Time carries me on as I ride
It just moves on as I abide
Keeps ticking on a steady stride
It's the course on which I glide.

Time has no end it seems to me
It will not bend it seems to be
A second lend would seem worthy
It cannot send it seems not free.

The cost is our life it's taken by time
No time for strife those mountains we climb
We throw out tripe its ticks do not rhyme
The end of our life still strutting is time.

Me and My Dog

Me and my dog in L.A.,
Ride along I-10 today,
We look out the window with nothing to say,
Then pick up our load to get out of L.A.,
We know we'll be back but we're done for today,
Me and my dog in L.A.

The Silhouettes

The silhouettes come alive at dawn,
Pink and gray, orange, purple, and blue are all around,
But the silhouettes come alive at dawn.

Chicken Scratches

My pen runs around like a chicken with its head cut off
    making scratches,
What's left, at times makes sense, at others it's just
    squiggly ink patches,
I try not to pay attention while it's running around,
I may not like what's coming out.
Just allowing it to bleed on the paper,
Sometimes its words to me cater.
Amazed at what it has inside,
I cut it loose and just let it glide.
Looking at the innards which the paper catches,
I can usually find more than chicken scratches.

Someone Said

Someone said, "You've lost your mind!"
"Oh no! That means I'm in a bind!
I hope again someday I'll find
That brilliant thing I call my mind!"

Lust Filled Eyes

Lust filled eyes follow you,
Do you feel the burn?
Hungry eyes ooze for you,
Do you absorb the flow?
Longing eyes watch all of you,
Do you feel the eerie sensation?

As I sit I watch him stare at you,
His eyes are screens his own.
As I sit he sees only you,
His focus is completely dissolved.
As I sit he's allured by you,
His eyes search for your soul.
As I sit he makes plans with you,
His eyes fulfill the mind.
As I sit I worry for you,
His eyes exclusively reveal.
Hungry, longing, lust filled eyes follow you,
Do you feel the burn,
Or is that intensity lost in void throughout the room?

Now and Then

I turned and saw her standing there
I looked again and she was gone.
She does that every now and then
Appearing for a moment to have not moved on.

I've seen her walking through the hall,
She closes doors to be left alone.
I feel her watching sometimes at night,
She stays around, this was her home.

The northeast room is the one she likes;
I hear her rocking in that old chair,
She stays in there most of the time
Still letting me know that she is there.

She doesn't scare me; that's not her style,
Though at times she sends a chill.
Unknown reason for why she's still around,
She just wants me to know that she is real.

Exorbitant Risk

They found two more today,
No chance to live their lives,
Children dead for no reason,
Murderous bastards – no punishment could possibly be
    enough.

Our society is ill,
Detached from reality,
Numb to perversion,
Unaffected by crime.

Our society accepts statistics when far away from ourselves,
Child molesters free to violate the innocent,
Rapists returned to their playgrounds,
Murderers left unpunished.

Children more vulnerable than an eagles prey,
Their world is filled with ominous predators.
So-called *justice* mandates to set them free,
Hunger survives to incite these perverted hunters.

Our society forsakes the innocent,
Self-righteous *adults* stuck on themselves.
Invented psychological disorders excusing criminality,
Making exorbitant risk the norm.

Children deserve to be protected,
Society has that obligation.
Despicable criminals should die,
Exoneration by psychology not condoned!

a thought

Humans humane?
Somewhat at times I question that.
Humane to animals, plants, and dirt maybe; not usually
    to other people…

The inhumanity of humanity,
Seclude the ugly,
Make fun of the obese,
Use abortion as birth control,
Discriminate against culture and race,
Mock the retarded,
Put down the different,
Oppress the weak,
Kick the incompetent,

Ignore the homeless,
Starve the hungry,
Maintain the terminally ill,
Kill the *Infidel*,
Murder for nothing at all,
Deem war necessary for survival,
Pit one against the other for personal gain,
Place the almighty dollar above all,
Eliminate integrity…
The mindset of humanity must change, or,
The mediocrity of humanity will become
The insanity of humanity which will eliminate
The chastity of humanity allowing
The inhumanity of humanity to become
The calamity of humanity.

The Silent Generation

The silent generation should speak.
Their stories are a history revered,
Their stories are a history which should never need be
    repeated.

Of one who spoke few words,
Sneaking around at night slitting throats and silently
    strangling,
Efforts to retain his own life and freedom,
Efforts to ensure American Freedom.

Another who speaks even less.
Horror so astounding,
Horror enough to make one's flesh creep,
Horror mortally terrorizing,
Packed in trains, starved, moved from camp to camp only
    hoping to be spared.
Surrendering for survival, fighting for life, praising God
    for Patton,
Regaining freedom himself while enduring many costs for
    ours.

Their lives in their eyes have all been humble,
Something they had to do; not heroic; not great; not worthy
    of praise,
No regrets, never questioning why, completely understood
    their purpose,
Answering the call their country needed, never desiring
    to speak of it again.
They do not seek the glory we wish to give.

I wish they would all speak.
Tell about the horrors of war,
Tell about the shrewdness of the enemy,
Tell about their fears,
Tell about their adaptiveness and resolve,
Tell about the things they had to do that haunt them still
    today,
Tell about their victories,
Tell about their losses,
Tell about their friends,
Tell about the good times which may have happened to sneak
    up on them in a most inopportune time in history,

Tell about the heartbreaks,
Tell us about fighting and winning the war.

Tell everything so we and our children will never forget,
Tell everything so all completely understand the sacrifices
    they made,
Tell everything so that America will not continue to take
    freedom for granted,
Tell everything so the courage to win again, if/when
    needed, can be found,
Tell everything in hopes that all of your efforts, your
    sacrifices, your blood, sweat, and tears, and your horrors
    may never need be relived again by those who follow.
Tell the world the ugly truth about war – every aspect
    – and dream in doing so that an effort like that will
    never ever need be undertaken again!

The silent generation is almost gone.
May the few who remain pour out their deepest secrets,
May they all be treated as the heroes they are,
America forever is grateful!

Minds Sight

The air is silent
The days been long,
I ponder the thoughts my eyes have seen,
I ponder the sights my mind has computed,
Totally confused, I reflect.

Portsmouth, Portland, Auburn and back through again,
Boston, Harvard, Worchester; onto Connecticut then.
Willington, Hartford, Watertown, and Danbury; cars all
the way through,
Fishkill in New York; a huge prison sits on the hill.
A river called Hudson runs down through the valley here,
Newberg and Maybrook are towns just west of there.
Cross the Delaware enroute to Pa.
Pocono Mountains to Scranton, Dupont, and Wilkes –
Barre,
Through Bloomsburg and Buckhorn to Milton where I
now sit.
The show through the windshield was impressive on this day,
The show in my mind now begins.

Today I missed swim lessons and baseball along with the
rest of summer's fun,
Tomorrow I'll miss his game and her laugh before my day
is done.
A golf ball, a boat, and of fish on a hook I dream,
Barbies, Hot Wheels, and Bratz go along with my summer
theme.
I envision my days with them at home a thousand miles
away,
The shows through the windshield are cool, but dreaming
of them is how I spend my day.

Note from a Trucker

Everyone around is in a hurry,
Non-stop everywhere I go,
Impatiently waiting in line,
Racing past only worried about themselves,
Tempers are short and gestures abundant,
My time to them not noticed.

Their schedule in life is all that exists,
Oblivious except as inconvenience,
I bring to them necessities,
I bring to them comforts,
I bring to them their race with "the Jones'",
I am the Rodney Dangerfield of the highway.

Their stress to me is noticed; mine to them is not,
Understanding by them is non-existent,
Patience lacks manifestation,
Courtesy is not an option,
Two seconds are all their lives are worth,
Stupidity around trucks is unforgiving.

(My dedication must be real,
My love for the road unceasing,
Though no longer a military soldier
My desire to serve the people remains.
These ungrateful highway idiots
Are the recipients of the goods I bring.)

Unknown to them, my day's been rough,
Bad directions led into a dead end – no way out,

Receiver said wait for door – five hours later was still there,

Shipper ticked 'cause I showed up for load,

Finally sent on way at five p.m. Monday,

Must be eight-hundred seventy-two miles by seven a.m. Tuesday,

Just ride around all day for no reason,

Just ride around all day to inconvenience you,

My day started at three a.m. Mon., will not end 'til maybe Tues. p.m.,

My day's not only been filled with traffic stresses,

My day's been spent with inconsiderate people ignorant to what I do just as you,

My day's been spent patiently controlling emotions so you have a chance to live while I drive.

If I acted as conceited as they, no one would survive,

If I was emotionally controlled as they, highway death would abound,

If impatience controlled me, their goods would cease to exist,

If I drove like they, their lives would be invaluable.

I'm not out here on vacation or solely for enjoyment; it is my accepted position in society,

Away from home more than not, I sacrifice the things you take for granted in service to you.

To New Poets

Pour your soul onto the page,
Bare your most inner thoughts,
Strip yourself of inhibitions,
Make yourself vulnerable to your reader.

Think not while you write,
Enter the page; with it become one,
Turn the paper into you,
Appear to those who follow.

Write, write, write!
Your mind is all that survives,
The pen sings life of you,
The poet who once was real.

Record your present surroundings,
Reflect on memories gone by,
Praise this country and God and Nature,
Sing of all people in definition of you.

Thus far, you've learned of me,
Expand now for generations to come,
My words in comparison are nothing,
It's you who shall continue the tradition!

Write, write, write!
Validate time; past, present, and future,
Validate those who came before,
Validate yourselves and inspire greatness in those who
    follow.

Write of all things both great and small,
Write of love and happiness; conquers and successes,
Write of hate and scorn; defeats and trials,
Define emotion; fill the page intimately.

You to come are the validation,
My era prepares for you just as the one before mine did me,
Your turn to pave the path forward,
Your turn to inform the future.

I will continue to sing,
I will reveal my time,
I will interpret the history before me,
I send it to you to explore.

Write, write, write!
Reflect on words you read,
Expand on the inspiration,
Write for all who follow you.

Constitutional?

Our Supreme Court overstepped,
An ownership society is now at risk,
Private Property is now available for political thieves,
Citizens' homesteads are now at stake,
Constitutional protection stripped away,
They should be impeached!

Whatever happened to Constitutional protection against illegal seizure of private property? (No longer is it illegal for the government)

It's bad enough it can be taken away for *public benefit*, now for *private benefit* and *tax revenue* too,

The Supreme Court seems to think Government as an institution is more important/valuable than the common citizen whose families' built (and continue to build) this country.

Shame on *the majority*!

They have completely lost touch with reality,

They completely ignore the Constitution of the United States,

They have no regard for the Bill of Rights (which was created exactly for this purpose in part),

They have become absolutely senile!

They do not serve the people justly.

Supreme Court Justices should not have lifetime appointments,

Supreme Court Justices should be forced to retire at a reasonable age,

Supreme Court Justices should be accountable to the people.

It is time the people set new precedent with impeachment.

There should be *checks* and *balances* on the Supreme Court.

Local governments have been abusing power for years,

Condemning property to devalue in order to steal it away from honest Americans,

Today, that is no longer even necessary,

Today, no longer do we have any recourse or appeal,
Today, our properties are no longer safe from political
        aspirations,
Today, America has changed,
Today, America the vision is less vivid,
Today, America, the reality, is fading,
Today, America the dream, struggles not to be sold out.

Shame, shame, shame on the Supreme Court,
Shame, shame, shame on them!
(Eminent Domain ruling (5-4) by U. S. Supreme Court)

Better Awaits

She came to me for real this time,
Concern filled her eyes and voice.
Worn out from life it's time for change,
Knowing better awaits.

Her mind is made for the change to come,
Her boys' reactions weigh down her soul,
They'll be alright from this change in time,
Knowing better awaits.

This time for real she came to me,
Seeking to know it will be ok,
It won't be easy but you will all get through,
Knowing better awaits.

Dismal

Alone I am trapped
I bounce off the walls inside my head
Toss and turn when I lay in bed
Dreary alone my way is drab
Alone I am trapped

Alone left only with thoughts
I recreate times when I felt not alone
Fade into the past to memories I own
Reaching alone for one thought to grab
Alone left only with thoughts

Alone I am trapped
I shake awake to find it's just me
Rollover and look with no one to see
Awaken alone again the day drab
Alone I am trapped

Pieces Scattered

Pieces of brokenness lie all around,
Jaggedness piercing to the sky,
Heart scattered as it pounds,
Fluttering lightly as butterflies,
Fear of pain known all too well,
Remembering the cloud from which it fell.

Thought

Thought it seems is the greatest race,
The part of life with a different face,
It can be trimmed with white lace
Or filled with Satan's eyes.

It comes upon you as you lie,
Toss and turn there is no tie,
To get away from before you die
Is but a thought itself.
They run around like busy elves,
The dust gets blown off old shelves,
Unknown time into they delve
And drive a man insane.

Avoid the thoughts which have a name,
Avoid the elves which play this game,
Avoid these fools or on you blame
The sleepless nights to come.

Twisted Faith

Adults not broken seemed to be the norm,
Normalness all around every Sunday morn,
Sheltered from reality transparent all around,
Each judging perfectly for Christ had been found.
Misguided actions tearing many lives in two,
Proclaiming, *Yes, He can save even you!*
It'd been easier to believe if they'd acted as they should
And allowed Him to save them, I'm sure that He could.

Hidden on Sunday's as the preacher would call
Dysfunction abounded once outside Church walls.
Reflection is fierce for it sheds a new light
On reasons why I strive to put out of sight
Their imperfection now found continuing in me
While proclaiming myself that I too have been saved by He.

Hypocrisy was normal as taught to the child
Learning how to deceive as we were beguiled,
Putting on a face to be what we think we should be,
Passing on their traits to continue through eternity.

A life of confusion now dominates as it leads,
A twisted faith inherited by observing *grownups* deeds.
These unbroken people now seem to have been ripped apart
With only a mask upon their defective, splintered hearts.

Higher

Not good enough, explained by she,
For someone so smart as he.
Tormentingly she convinces her mind
He's too good for someone like her to find.
Who am I that he chooses to love me?
Why am I so fortunate to have one like he?

She loves him yet felt she was better when they were young,
He loves her and felt that together they would forever belong.
Racing through time and advancing in life,
Surpassing some dreams, conquering strife,
Together through time they continue to ride,
Yet now he's better, so she tries to step aside.

He's not that way; himself he sees's not higher,
Together they forged through challenges to retire.
A team they've been through all of these years,
Through fun and trials and all the painful tears,
To get to the point where they are today,
Together forever, come what may.

An Act

Tired of pretending, I don't give a damn anymore.
People are mostly phony, including me.

We make ourselves self righteous
All the while striving not to be a bore,
We sell ourselves as something
While trying to disguise the whore,
We sell ourselves to people
Doing one's best to declare we're more,
We cheat ourselves of life,
We lose sight of who we are.

Why sell ourselves as something
When we know it's all an act?
Why tell ourselves we are
Without support of fact?
Why make believe to all
We're more than what they lack?
Why lie and lie and lie
And with the Devil pact?

A human game not fake
Is what I think should moor.

Culture so it's not deceptive
Leaving people to long no more.

(No Title)

There must be a greater purpose for our being here on
  earth;
Otherwise our lives are pointless.
The constellations stand together in formation
Holding the secrets which comprise the universe they
  are.
Truth is at our fingertips and always has been,
It will continue to be until change permeates the night sky;
  even then it may only change what we will come to
  know (and who's to say then it would be different?).

WWIII

Tensions rising,
Russia, Iran, Europe, China, Israel, United States,
Foreseeable future disaster,
Not so distant conflict,
War of the world,
Devastation unavoidable,
Difference irresolvable without force,
First shots of words have been fired,
Retraction not a believable option
Action at hand,
The machine is moving,
War now inevitable,
Most frightening reality most likely will become real,

Massive number nuclear rockets fly,
The earth will quake,
Will humans survive our own actions?
Will anything be left to live for?
Can this be stopped before it advances?
Outlook unfavorable,
The men of the world will clash,
Cultures warring for real,
Civilization uncivil,
US surround's Iran,
Israel to defend its own by attacking,
Escalation worldwide the result,
War for all again.

Fear

True fear is frightenly real,
Shaking your body the quivers you feel,
Beside yourself you heel.
Cold sweaty hands unable to be controlled,
Cupping together so your eyes they can hold
While trying to pressure your mind to be bold.
The fear surrounds without any substance
Formulating the sound which now the mind chants
Bringing insanity to the dance.
Justified is only some fear;
As of people and governments; the real beasts here,
And others which present themselves clear.
Fiction can manifest as somewhat real,
Enough to escape reason and with it steal
Comfort and security making fear surreal.

(No Title)

A classic novel fits like a snug, warm glove in winter. It blocks the shrill, cutting north wind and warms your bones while the rest of the world around you freezes. The words release you from reality, temporarily allowing a marvelous, cozy escape from a present day blast of a bitterly, subzero, winter-like culture.

Non-Statesmen

Politics are about the Politicians,
Raising money, obtaining votes and congratulations,
Forgetting about the true business of the State,
Self absorbed, yet driving a nation to its fate.

Continual Spin

I turn in my head from here to there;
I spin around with vision unclear,
I reach for a thought which is dear.

One I grab which was long ago
The next I try to remember slow
Before it brings to time of woe.
Lost for which thought I wish to relive
I struggle to search the now.
New life appears upon the scene
We train and teach for them to know how

To decide their way through life.
Some passed through time with abundance to give
Sharing the knowledge they've seen.
Others learned all about strife
Teaching somehow not to go.
Others and others, yet others again
Before us all, they all have been
To pass the torch as they knew when.
Bearing the burden of raising the next
Almost it seems we're hexed.
Caught in time the same perplexed
We and new must go.
Maybe none will ever know
The best of which how to live,
Maybe all are doomed to turn
On the memory of lessons we learn.

(No Title)

To delineate the Ideal;
Seems to me surreal.
Alexis claims it must be real
For a poet to be ideal.

A Hold

Staring into the night
Stirring inside with fright
Of what is in the dark for me.
What it is I cannot see.

Unsure of what lurks behind the pitch
And what will unfold as the next big glitch
I stare into the night
And allow hold to be taken by fright.

Impediment

Temporarily insane;
Must kick start my mind again
And let the words pour out as rain
As to leave not my promise in vain.
It's the pen which has been hiding;
That's right, blame the pen for not abiding,
Not taking time to perform any writing,
As to impede paper and mind in confiding.

Imagine US

Oh to write once more with passion.
The realm of mind is an unlimited ration
Of thought, made just for paper.
The vastness of unrestricted imagination
Combined with the spaciousness of our great nation
Is enough for words to never taper.

I Pray

…I pray the Lord my soul to keep…
May He comfort all while we sleep…

This night the family tosses and turns
Hoping her fight with Hell will lessen its churn
And she will gain the upper hand.
May God's hand wrap around,
May she feel His love abound
And kick her demons to the ground;
May she learn again to stand.

A fight unfair is tough.
The oppressor is one who plays rough.
A stranglehold around its neck
Is all it needs to place in check
The victim who soon becomes consumed;
Addicted to singing its numbing tune.

Fight, dammit, and knock it out!
Evict its hold during this bout
And come back to us as you!
Watching this fight has made us blue,
Confusion and anger are common to us all
As to the bottom we've watched you fall.

Tomorrow night we'll toss and turn
Waiting for good we wish to learn.
Again we'll fight with sleep 'til morn
Knowing your night will be rough and torn.
We're with you in our separate towns
Hoping a smile will soon replace your frown.

Understand you're not alone.
We are affected in our homes.
We fight your fight with you here,

We struggle emotionally with your there,
We cry and pray then cry some more…
We scream and pray and cry even more…
Tears then hope then more tears pour…
Struggle in thought and hit the floor…
We scream and pray and cry some more…

…I pray the Lord my soul to keep…
May He comfort all while we sleep…

Dear God

To God I write a note
As my mind is all afloat
In thought.

What I write is yet to be
For all it is I know you'll see
A thought.

Inside there is a book
A glimpse, to you a look
At thought.

God knows the thought
So a note there's not,
Just thought.

Heart and Soul

I bared my soul for you to see
Instead, away you stole it from me.
I wonder if I will ever trust again
I strive to be whole; I only wonder when.

I trusted my heart for you to hold,
I gave it to you before you turned cold,
I wonder if it ever again will be one,
I wonder if before my days are done.

Naked and shattered I wander about
For glue and clothing; by love I doubt
For cold I am as learned from you
I walk and search while blue.

Thank you for ripping my world apart
It forced me to search for and find my heart
You never had it; twas an illusion from me
Still beating strong for a true love to see.

My soul, I'm learning, is still within
Never stolen away; only drowned in gin
By the pain that was caused when I thought you took all
But now I see and again can stand tall.

Smile

Pure beauty lies in her smile
True happiness shines through her eyes;
If only her smile would last more than a while,
We wouldn't have to watch as she dies.

This Old Pocket Knife

By accident I found this envelope today;
Says it is addressed to me.
I wondered what the inside could have to say,
So I opened it up to see…

Memories of the "Old Timer" came flooding back then…
I remembered the day it arrived
I must have been twice more than five
One of the biggest steps of my life,
The day I got this old pocket knife.
This Old Pocket Knife
Falling back in the couch with that old knife in hand
Looking back to days of then.
The adventures we had from water to land
Taking me back to days of when…

Memories of the "Old Timer" came flooding back then…
The day my finger bled like a sieve,
A scar on my leg it did leave,
One of the biggest days of young life,
The day I got this old pocket knife.

I just laughed as I thought how proud I was that day
Then wandered out to whittle.
It sliced my thumb then on the ground the knife lay,
Reliving when I was little…

Memories of the "Old Timer" came flooding back then…
I remembered the day it arrived
I must have been twice more than five
One of the biggest steps of my life,
The day I got this old pocket knife.

The day my finger bled like a sieve,
A scar on my leg it did leave,
One of the biggest days of young life,
The day I got this old pocket knife.

The Intelligent

If we are the intelligent species here
Why haven't we learned from the passing years?
We as man continue to abhor,
And we as nations still war.

Drive

They drive to where they want to be;
Work, church, or home; their sanctity.
I watch them as they go.
It's late at night; they should already be there,

At home I mean; with the people who care
About those whom they know.
Yet those alone with nowhere to be,
Those on vacation and commuters like me
Aim through the night down the row.
Somewhere in time someday they'll arrive
And find that before they were not alive,
Just driving as if lost in the snow.
Until that day they drive
Hoping to be revived
By people; friend not foe.

(No Title)

Rain froze here when it fell,
Made my head ring like a bell.
Mud would've been more kind,
Only my shoes would I have needed to find.

(No Title)

Be real with zeal, be real
No time to act, be real
Pretend is fine in times unreal
But grown men must be real

<u>Simple</u>

Who am I that keeps you hanging on every word?
My words are simple,
My words are common,
My words are not unique.
Who are you that keeps striving to read more?
You are not simple,
You are not common,
You are unique.
Well then, read on.
I bolster you for you are the future,
I sing of me for I am now,
I praise days gone by for they set this stage.

Others before me defined my time,
Invention, victory, suffering, dreams,
They pushed forward and finished their scene
Passing it on to simplify mine.

My time breaks new ground,
Equality, political correctness, sensitivity,
Pushing the envelope further to absurdity
Making sameness all around.

Speak out against indifference!
Encourage individualism,
Understand there are smart,
There are dumb,
There are common.
Understand people are not all the same!
Experiences differ,

Colors viewed are not equal,
Opinions are unique to all.

There are great, there are not,
There are kind, there are not,
There are carefree, there are not,
There are educated, there are not,
There are confused.
People's problems are unique to themselves,
People's solutions vary.
Loneliness is the only thing common to all.
You are connected to me through mind,
The answers you seek I cannot find,
Your heart and mine together bleed,
I will always write, and you will read.

Do I Wish

Do I wish to be a Poet for America today?
It seems the dream is fading, or is it gone?

Place me in a time a hundred years back to dream about
    the way things could be today.
Then, the dream was beaming with life eternal,
It was forging forward without limit,
It was unhindered by frightened politicians,
The people yet had faith in themselves enough to dream.

Is our country now fearful of dreaming…or is it just
    encumbered?
What has stifled the dream of being free?
Fear?

Fear is what created the dream; it is what made it real!
It is what has kept this country Free!
Fear of being ruled,
Fear of being imprisoned unjustly,
Fear of being quieted,
Fear of Tyranny,
Fear of not being able to live!
That should be enough to desire to maintain our freedoms
    – not what causes us to turn them over.

We should be demanding less constraint by bureaucracy,
Less control by government,
Less cowardice in those elected,
Less bickering in Washington,
Less ignorance in ourselves.
We should be demanding the ability again to dream while
    awake – we would then live the dream which is America!
Fear is useful but it's becoming impedimenta for us all.

Yes, I wish to be a Poet for America today, if for nothing
    else, to ensure the dream survives!

The Society

The society of which I will belong is that of *Dead Poets*.
Writing while here I proclaim their insight;
Sun, stars, space; Clouds, rain, snow;
Plants, animals, life! People, culture, society;
Politics, war, peace; Suffering, murder, death;
Justice.

Their thoughts on paper have survived,
People still try to understand them.
Their minds worked in incomprehensible ways,
They gave their *power* to their pen.

Some rhymed, some chose not to, and others just had no
meter at all,
Yet each and every last one of them gave in to a higher call.
They wrote for fun; they wrote with meaning;
They wrote to leave their mark,
They wrote with conviction; they wrote with curiosity;
They wrote with a passion from deep within their soul.

They breathed their words onto their page
So we could see their stage.
They took a chance with the pen immortalizing their
opinions,
So we – removed this far away – could see what they were
thinking.
They found the things that we take for granted and made
each one significant,
They praised the things that were all around to make us
think today.

They followed life and they followed death not only to
observe,
They followed life and they followed death to show us it's
not absurd.
They loved the rivers and the plains, the mountains and
the sea,
They loved the people and the trains; they had a love for
you and me,

Had they not, they would not have cared to write down
all their thoughts,
Had they not the words they left, the past would be for not.

They wrote about things in their present which still relate
today,
The words they wrote in their time are quoted by us this day.
They wrote to the poor; they wrote to the rich; they wrote
to you and me,
They wrote of love; they wrote of hate; they wrote of all
humanity.

If only my words will be read that well I then will have
succeeded,
For Great like them I long to be, with my words again
repeated.
I hope someday before I'm dead my writing will be revealed,
So you today can see the thoughts from yesterday unsealed.

But even so, the society of which I will belong is that of
Dead Poets.